Y0-BYL-655

ENDORSEMENTS

"George Kops is one of the outstanding coaches in this business. You should read his book — *Great Speakers Aren't Born* captures the real essence of the presentation process. A good read."
— **William Miller**
  President, Otis NAO

"A unique process for developing your presentation skills."
— **Frank Parisi**
  Vice President Communications, Cowles Media Company

"Our way of doing business has been fundamentally changed as a result of work we have done with George Kops. The concepts they have provided for effective communication to our clients and prospects has been extremely effective in our efforts to grow and develop our business."
— **Matt Simmons**
  President, Simmons & Company International

"Kops and Worth have packaged the key ingredients for developing presentations your listeners will remember."
— **Curt Linke**
  Vice President Communications, Carrier Corporation

GREAT SPEAKERS AREN'T BORN

The Complete Guide to Winning Presentations

- *Master the art of giving great speeches*
- *Learn the trade secrets of the great speakers*
- *Obtain expert advice from Fortune 500 training consultants*
- *Build audience rapport, handle questions and answers, and use visuals*

GEORGE KOPS AND RICHARD WORTH

Lifetime Books, Inc.
Hollywood, Florida
800-771-3355
http: www//lifetimebooks.com
e-mail: lifetime@shadow.net

Copyright © 1996 by George Kops and Richard Worth
New Edition 1997

All rights reserved. Published by Lifetime Books, Inc., 2131 Hollywood Blvd., Holly-wood, FL 33020.

Reproduction, translation, or use in any form by any means of any part of this work beyond that permitted by Section 107 or 108 of the 1976 United States Copyright Act without the permission of the copyright owner is unlawful. Requests for permission or further information should be addressed to the Permissions Department, Lifetime Books, Inc., 2131 Hollywood Boulevard, Hollywood, FL 33020.

This publication is designed to provide accurate and authoritative information in regard to the subject matter covered. It is sold with the understanding that the publisher is not engaged in rendering legal, accounting, or other professional service. If legal advice or other assistance is required, the services of a competent professional person should be sought. *From A Declaration of Principles jointly adopted by a Committee of the American Bar Association and a Committee of Publishers.*

To order additional copies of *Great Speakers Aren't Born*, please send a check or money order for $14.95 (plus $3.00 shipping/handling) to: Lifetime Books, Inc. 2131 Hollywood Blvd., Hollywood, FL 33020. Please write to us to receive a free catalog and information on upcoming books that interest you.

Library of Congress Cataloging-in Publication Data

Kops, George, 1938—
    Great speakers aren't born : how to develop winning presentations
  / by George Kops & Richard Worth.
        p. cm.
    Based on seminars developed by Focus Communications International.
    ISBN 0-8119-0841-0 (pbk.)
    1. Public speaking. 2. Oral communication. 3. Business presentations.
  I. Worth, Richard. II. Title. III. Title: Great speakers aren't born.
  PN4121.K934   1996
  808.5'1--DC20
                                    96-26857
                                        CIP

10 9 8 7 6 5 4 3 2
Design by Vicki Heil
Printed in Canada

TABLE OF CONTENTS

Foreword .... **ix**

Introduction .... **xi**

Chapter One — Approaching the Starting Line 1
• *Remember the 8 key points of successful presentations*
• *Add the 7 Cs to your next talk: commitment, creativity, clarity,*
  coherence, conciseness, correctness and credibility
• *Be prepared to work hard at becoming a better speaker*

Chapter Two — At the Starting Gun 13
• *Organize your talk around a central message*
• *Make your message meaningful to the audience*
• *Conduct a listener analysis*

Chapter Three — Out of the Blocks 27
• *Ideas are the stuff of successful presentations*
• *Include ideas that support your central message*
• *Anecdotes and examples bring a talk to life*

WITHDRAWN

v

JAN - 1998

Chapter Four — Leaping the Hurdles 41
• *A tightly organized talk will be more meaningful to listeners*
• *Use one of several organizing patterns for your presentation*
• *Develop an outline for your talk*

Chapter Five — Finding an Opening 61
• *Use an effective opening or listeners will tune out*
• *Relate the opening to the central message*
• *Keep the opening brief*

Chapter Six — Strategy for Success 75
• *Use the 3Ts to structure presentations: tell the audience what you want to tell them; tell them; then tell them again*
• *Organizing patterns help you develop the body of a talk*
• *The conclusion enables you to reiterate your central message*

Chapter Seven — Visualize Your Way to Victory 91
• *You are your most important visual aid*
• *Keep visuals simple and brief*
• *Use only a minimum of visuals*

Chapter Eight — Mastering the Give &Take 107
• *Begin a dialogue with your audience*
• *Open-ended questions are excellent for audience involvement*
• *Q&A sessions also encourage listener participation*

Chapter Nine — Energy for the Long Run 123
• *Use energy to develop enthusiasm in your listeners*
• *Vocal skills add energy*
• *Body language also enhances a talk*

Chapter Ten — Practice Pays Off 135
• *A rehearsal enables you to perfect your talk*
• *Make sure your central message is clear*
• *Practice your visual and vocal skills*

Chapter Eleven — A Winning Presentation 149
• *Make sure your talk fits the allotted time*
• *Channel your stage fright into energy for your talk*
• *Check the equipment in advance*

Chapter Twelve — Special Topics: Video Conferencing And Voice Mail 157
• *The key to successful video-conferencing is preparation*
• *Use all the elements of Value Added Communications® in video-conferencing*
• *Energy makes voice mail messages more effective*

Appendix 173
• *Planning Exercise • Presentation Planner • Ideas & Informaton*
• *Outline for Your Presentation • Opening for Your Presentation*
• *Practice Exercise • Conclusion for Your Presentation*
• *Visual Aid Planner • Practice Exercise • Dialogue Questions*
• *Q&A Preparation*

Glossary 183

Bibliography 185

Index 187

Today, the art of effective communication is critical for business success and is truly the competitive edge.

The right presentation can spell the difference between success and failure in the effort to achieve your goals.

At Focus Communications International, we work with our clients in "helping to build your business through better personal communications."

For additional information on our services, contact us at:
tel: (203) 966-0282
fax: (203) 966-1949
e-mail: georgekops@aol.com
internet:http://www.focuscommunications.com

FOREWORD

Perhaps you have had the experience of listening to a very dynamic speaker and thinking: "I wish I could speak that effectively." Then, almost immediately, you tell yourself: "Oh, that is a gift; I could never be that good!"

Well, you can. Scores of managers in my organization have become successful speakers. They found the process not only enjoyable, but also extremely rewarding. Suddenly, they could make better sales presentations; they could run better meetings; and some of them even reported receiving a standing ovation after they finished addressing an audience. Nothing could be more satisfying.

Each of these managers shared several characteristics. At one time, they had lacked confidence in themselves as public speakers and, by their own admission, they often delivered presentations that seemed to "fall flat" with their audiences. How could they improve?

Each of them participated in the Value Added Communications program, which was given by Focus Communications International to our organization. Managers who used to stand stiffly in front of an audience learned how to inject far more energy into their deliveries by transforming their speaking style. Others learned how to give their talks more focus and how to actively involve their listeners in a presentation, applying techniques that made them much better speakers.

There is no magic to these things. They are practical, common-sense approaches that anyone can apply. But their impact is enormous. Managers who participate in the Focus process experience the satisfaction of making tremendous improvement, an improvement that occurs so rapidly it almost seems like magic. And the more they work and participate in the program, the more they benefit from it.

In *Great Speakers Aren't Born: The Complete Guide to Winning Presentations*, the techniques of Value Added Communications are now made easily accessible to everyone. If you read the material in this book, do the practice exercises, and complete the worksheets to prepare for your next presentation, you can become a more success-ful speaker.

This book takes you on a thoroughly satisfying journey, one that will enable you to reap immediate benefits in both your professional and personal life. By mastering a few oral communications skills, you can express your ideas more effectively, achieve greater influ-ence among your friends and co-workers, and stand out as someone who really does make a difference. All of these goals are well worth achieving.

— Richard Sloan
  President
  United Technologies Automotive, Europe

INTRODUCTION

BECOMING A BETTER SPEAKER

Paraphrasing a well-known aphorism, "Great speakers aren't born, they're made," this book shows you how to become, if not a great speaker, at least a much better one.

Great Speakers Aren't Born is based on the state-of-the-art seminars developed by Focus Communications International. We have trained thousands of executives at some of the world's best known organizations. For more than a decade, these programs have enabled participants to become better professionals, better managers and better leaders.

Today, communications skills are particularly important in charting a course for the employees in your organization or your department. In an age of accelerating change and increasing uncertainty, people are looking for clear direction, and you can provide it. Whether you are shaping a new vision, spearheading an initiative into an untried market, speaking to the media, or simply conducting a business meeting, effective public speaking is frequently the margin of difference between success and failure.

Great Speakers Aren't Born has two overriding objectives. First, we teach you the presentation skills necessary to becoming a better speaker. Second, the book provides an opportunity for you to practice these skills as you prepare your next presentation. Every chapter contains exercises and worksheets that will carry you through the presentation planning process. You can use these forms to evaluate your current skill level, gather information, develop an outline for your presentation, write a powerful introduction, create visual aids and rehearse your delivery. (Additional copies of the forms are in the Appendix of the book.)

In addition, a number of chapters contain sample talks which may serve as valuable models for your next presentation. Each speech highlights important elements that illustrate the material presented in the chapter.

Great Speakers Aren't Born opens with a discussion of eight key points to consider as you start to prepare a presentation, including an evaluation of your verbal, visual and vocal skills. In Chapter Two, the book emphasizes the importance of developing a main idea, or central message, that will make a significant impact on your audience. This is the most critical step in developing your talk. Our central message is that improved speaking skills can be learned. What this means is that as you improve your skills, you will be more effective in your professional and personal life. Indeed, your ability to communicate well is your most important asset. All the information you have in your head is of no value to others until you communicate it in an interesting and meaningful fashion.

Chapter Three examines the process of brainstorming ideas and collecting anecdotes and examples to bring them to life for your audience, while Chapter Four presents a variety of organizational patterns that you can use to structure the ideas in your presentation. The next two chapters focus on developing an opening for your talk that hooks the audience. We show how to ensure that the body of your speech is clear and concise, and that it finishes with a powerful closing.

Visual aids can play a significant role in presenting complex information. Chapter Seven looks at various types of visual media, such as overheads, slides, computers, and video, and explains how to create powerful visual aids. The following chapter is devoted to improving your ability to interact with an audience by developing a dialogue with them and conducting effective Q&A sessions. We also discuss how to handle questions asked by the media.

Chapter Nine explains how to infuse energy into your delivery through visual skills, such as eye contact and body language, as well as vocal skills, like the advantages of pauses and the proper level of pacing.

Rehearsing a talk will usually allow you to eliminate any major flaws, and Chapter Ten enables you to evaluate your rehearsal in terms of verbal, vocal and visual skills.

Chapter Eleven contains tips for conquering such problems as stage fright, interruptions, and schedule changes. The final chapter looks at important special topics, such as video-conferencing and voice mail.

Many surveys indicate that most people are not listening to the words being spoken at business meetings. The listeners' minds are wandering because the speakers have not made their talk interesting and relevant for the audience. Indeed, the speakers often confess they do not know how to make the material engaging. They often feel frustrated because they're not great "natural" speakers. They see good speaking as a natural skill, one they do not possess and cannot acquire. As a result, their presentations are significantly less effective than they should be.

Great speakers aren't born — they are trained. They work to develop their skills and become much better at speaking. You can also improve your skills. But it takes adequate preparation — that is the key to any successful presentation. Underlying all the information in this book is a single line of advice: "Do not leave it until the last minute." Give yourself plenty of time to prepare and use all of the steps presented in every chapter. They have not been included on a whim or to make the process of speech making needlessly difficult. They are based on practical experience. They work! Students in Focus Communications seminars have used them repeatedly and reported tremendous success in delivering presentations.

George Kops is the president of Focus Communications International. Kops and the company teach the concepts of Value Added Communications® and how to apply them in a wide variety of speaking situations. Kops has worked with many large clients, including GE, IBM, Glaxo Wellcome, United Technologies and MCI, helping their executives become better speakers. Today, these professionals are successfully utilizing their oral communication skills in sales presentations, acquisition proposals, board of director meetings, media appearances, and in many other settings.

Richard Worth is a professional business writer and author of ten books. He has also produced several hundred video presentations for Fortune 500 corporations. Additionally, Worth presents writing seminars for Focus Communications International.

EDITOR'S STATEMENT

If the old adage is true, "It's not what you know, but who you know," then it is certainly true, "It's not just what you say, but also how you say it." To achieve great oratory skills means you have achieved success. Once you have mastered the ability to speak and present in a convincing manner, you have mastered your fate.

Great Speakers Aren't Born is the complete guide to winning presentations, written by two communications professionals, each with twenty years of experience in making the spoken word work for them. If you want to improve your ability to convince an audience, no matter the size, of anything you are saying, please read this book. Even seasoned lecturers will pick up valuable pointers.

The art of great speech-giving is a gift that can be learned. Here is a proven approach that will allow you to create successful presentations. As a result, you will become a better manager, a better professional, a better leader.

Scientists have yet to discover a gene that people are born with that gives someone the natural ability to hold an audience of 300 people in the palm of their hand. No, great speakers aren't born but they can be developed. All the training you will ever need can be found in this book.

Great Speakers Aren't Born is based on the state-of-the-art seminars developed by Focus Communications International, which has trained thousands of executives at the world's best known organizations. They have developed a system that centers around the seven C's: commitment, creativity, clarity, coherence, conciseness, correctness and credibility.

Instruction in the skills necessary to become a better speaker are offered in detail. Now you can learn the trade secrets of all great speakers! If you want to see some startling results, just videotape your next presentation — before reading this book. Then, after just one reading of *Great Speakers Aren't Born*, go out and tape your next presentation. You are guaranteed to see a marked difference in your ability to captivate audiences and get them to believe in what you are saying.

Remember, great speakers aren't born and it is never too late to develop and improve your speaking skills. Good luck!

— Senior Editor
  Brian Feinblum

DEDICATION

To Ginny, George Ali, Greg, and Karen.

CHAPTER ONE

APPROACHING THE STARTING LINE

Highlights

- *Remember the 8 key points of successful presentations*
- *Add the 7 Cs to your next talk*
- *Be prepared to work hard at becoming a better speaker*

A manager at a large manufacturing plant has been asked to prepare a brief presentation on self-managed work teams. He wants to talk about the success of the teams in his area, which handle purchasing. But at a meeting of all the team leaders, nobody can agree on a simple message that summarizes what they have accomplished.

"There's too much material here," one of them says.

"How can we boil it all down?" another person asks.

As the meeting adjourned, they still had not come up with any answers. Two weeks went by, the group gathered for another meeting, but there was very little progress. The deadline for the presentation was now only a few days away.

1

"We've got to do something!" the manager said, pounding the table. But nobody offered any suggestions.

Finally, the manager decided to put a talk together by himself. The evening before the presentation, he burned the midnight oil and wrote out a long, rambling speech, hoping it would make sense.

But, standing in front of his audience the next day, he could barely keep his hands from shaking. He started with what he thought was an amusing story. Unfortunately, no one laughed. And his talk went downhill from there. It was a nightmare.

How many of us have awakened in a cold sweat from a nightmare like the one that overtook this manager? Or, even worse, actually lived it? A manager's ability to stand up and make a successful presentation can often make the critical difference between success and failure. As one engineer put it: "If you are a manager of a group, not only must you get people to work for you effectively, you have to get your thoughts across to the rest of the organization. They need to know what your message is and why your group is important. If you are going to get funded in your area, you have to make presentations to capital appropriations committees. It is just part of the job."

Whether you are trying to create an impact on top management or persuade the members of your staff to embrace your vision, you must communicate effectively. As corporations eliminate layers of hierarchy and empower employees, managers can no longer rely solely on their authority to get anything accomplished. They must be skilled in using the power of words in a variety of situations, from small, informal team meetings to major marketing and sales campaigns. This chapter looks at eight key points to consider as you start to think about your next presentation.

1. UNDERSTAND THE PURPOSE
OF PRESENTATIONS

It is easy to look on the task of preparing a presentation only from your own point of view, as something that "I" have to do. But unless you are writing in a diary or a journal, every communication that you produce involves an audience. The purpose of your communication is to reach those listeners. In some instances, you may be trying to simply pass along information. But in many other cases, your goal is far more ambitious: It is to persuade them of your point of view. In their book *Beyond The Hype, Rediscovering The Essence of Management*, Robert Eccles and Nitin Nohria explain that the basic task of managers "is to mobilize action by using language creatively." Persuading others to take action as the result of a talk that you delivered is a powerful skill to possess.

Ask yourself: Am I simply trying to inform my audience and explain something to them? Or am I standing up there to persuade the audience that my information is correct and they should act on it? It would be wonderful if all you had to do was present your data and the sheer brilliance of it would be enough to convince your audience. Usually it takes far more. As one executive put it: "We all have to sell ideas." Therefore, you must always prepare a presentation with the audience in mind by asking yourself: What will convince them, what will move them to action, what will they remember?

2. MAKE IT MEMORABLE AND YOU
WILL BE REMEMBERED

John F. Kennedy is considered one of the greatest American orators of the 20th century. If you have ever listened to a classic Kennedy speech, you realize it is not only his words but his delivery that make it memorable. Kennedy's vocal skills—the change of tempo and volume, for example, as well as the visual image of the man helped make some of his speeches forever memorable.

While your next presentation on the company's new quality initiative or re-engineering program may not reach the summit that Kennedy sometimes attained, it need not be a boring monologue that sends your audience off to sleep. Instead of settling for a second class talk that will be forgotten almost as soon as you leave the podium, set a higher standard for yourself and your audience will more likely remember what you said.

 ## 3. ACCENTUATE YOUR ASSETS, MINIMIZE YOUR DEFICIENCIES

As one of the students in our seminars explained: "If you perceive you're good at public speaking, then you might want to do more of it. I think I am pretty rusty and I had a couple of bad experiences."

Many people would just as soon avoid the necessity of making a presentation, because they believe they are not any good at it, or at least not as good as someone else. That may be. But the truth probably is that you possess some significant strengths as a speaker as well as some other skills that could stand improving. Perhaps you are very effective at crafting the words to present an idea, but your delivery could best be described as a slow, halting monotone. Or perhaps you are a whiz when it comes time to stand up and speak on your feet, using your hands to generate enthusiasm, but you do not spend enough time in preparation, and sometimes "winging it" trips you up.

Throughout this book we will be discussing three main types of presentation skills: verbal, visual and vocal. *Verbal skills* include such things as defining the main idea of your talk, conducting research, developing the contents of your presentation, creating visual aids, handling dialogue, and question and answer sessions. *Visual skills* refer to the effective use of gestures and facial expressions to reinforce your words, as well as how to maintain eye contact with your listeners. Finally, *vocal skills* include pacing, pauses, and changes of tone and volume as you deliver your presentation.

Based on a self-analysis, list your assets and deficiencies as a speaker:

ASSETS   DEFICIENCIES

VERBAL SKILLS

VISUAL SKILLS

VOCAL SKILLS

What is your strongest presentation skill?

_____

What is your weakest presentation skill?

_____

How could you improve this skill?

_____

How do you think the audience rates you as a speaker?_____

How do you rate yourself?

_____

"Cut it in half, get it straight, and leave out the damn jokes! — Lyndon B. Johnson

4. THERE IS NO GAIN WITHOUT
SOME PAIN

Students in Focus Communications seminars will be the first to admit that the process of improving their presentation skills can be tough, frustrating and, yes, even painful. But nothing worth doing is any different. If you have ever tried to lose weight, stop smoking, or learn to play a musical instrument, then you know what we mean. As one student put it: "It's just like golf. If you want to get better, you have to work at it."

You have to work at speaking well too, but it is much easier than golf. And many others have succeeded before you. Probably one of the first great orators was Demosthenes, who overcame a terrible stutter by speaking with pebbles in his mouth while walking along the shores of Greece. Lee Iaccoca, for example, honed his effective presentation style through hours of practice and perseverance.

Surveys of the top leadership training programs in the country, programs which have graduated thousands of managers, show that most of them include practice exercises in some form of presentation skills. In many of these programs, managers work on developing their own visions for the future, communicating them to others, and enlisting their support. They also learn how to influence and motivate their peers. No doubt, some managers find these experiences uncomfortable, but most graduates report that the training enables them to reap the benefits of successful speaking.

5. FOCUS ON THE BIG BENEFITS
OF EFFECTIVE SPEAKING

You achieve a higher profile. Your success as a public speaker can give you additional prominence within your organization. In the era of downsizing when everyone's future seems open to question, the more value you bring to your company, the more likely you are to retain your position there. Do not simply assume that you will be noticed by your superiors for the sheer incisiveness of your ideas. The fact is: What you say is no more important than how well you say it.

You achieve your goals. Communication skills are one of the key attributes of every effective manager. In an article for *The New York Times*, Doron Levin described all-star quarterback Joe Montana as the epitome of successful management. On the football field, he had the ability to inspire confidence, to focus on the task before him, and to communicate with the other members of his team to ensure the next play was executed properly.

What good does it do to kill yourself developing a new plan or proposal only to see it misunderstood by the other people on your team simply because you did not communicate it to them clearly? Or suppose you've spent weeks on a program to turn around your department and then it is rejected because you lacked the skill to explain it persuasively to your superiors?

Do not short-change the importance of your presentations. They are just as critical in winning support for your ideas as the ideas themselves.

Your audience benefits. You cannot forget the audience. They are usually the ones you want to help through your presentation. Whether you are speaking to a group of employees about a new safety program or a gathering of concerned citizens in your community about the advantages of a proposed recreation center, your goal is to benefit them.

You increase your own sense of satisfaction. Whether seeking to improve your position at work, win approval of your pet plan, or provide a service to your audience, all of these things can be derived from effective speaking. But you will also have the satisfaction of knowing that you have mastered an essential skill that makes you more effective at doing your job.

In her book, *Becoming A Manager*, Linda Hill describes the experiences of new managers as they learned the ropes. After only a few months, she explains, they were "describing people management as communication and saying communication skills were vital." If you want to be effective on the job, you must communicate successfully.

 ## 6. LET YOURSELF GO

Are you someone who generally stands locked behind the podium during a talk, reading from your notes in a dull monotone? Or perhaps your presentations consist of a towering pile of overhead transparencies which you project on the screen, one after the other, reading each of them word for word to the audience?

If you have repeated this approach often enough, it has probably become fairly monotonous for you by now, say nothing of the effect it has on your listeners. While there is a certain security in doing something the same way all the time, change can offer you several advantages. By altering the style of your presentation, you can create a new challenge for yourself, add more interest to the task of preparation, more zest to your delivery, and wake up your audience by surprising them with the way you present your next talk. If your goal is not to be noticed or remembered, stick to that old ho-hum method of giving a presentation. But if you want to stand out, then consider doing things better.

This does not mean that we want to turn you into a sports announcer like Dick Vitale, wildly gesturing at your audience and making the most routine occasion into a major event. Your corporate culture probably would not accept this approach, anyway. Besides, it will make you feel uncomfortable to be someone you're not. But we believe that everyone has the ability to improve their speaking style. At best, this will only involve amplifying your natural style while you deliver your presentations.

If you have been gripping the podium like a security blanket, try leaving it behind the next time you speak. Walk around in front of your listeners and speak to them directly without the barrier of a lectern. Your talk will immediately tend to become more dynamic and intimate. The audience will respond better to you, which will add more pleasure to your own experience of public speaking.

If you are an "overhead junkie," throw away that pile of transparencies. You can probably give that presentation without them. Let the audience focus on you and what you want to say to them. You are the most effective visual aid you can ever present.

As you prepare for your next presentation, let yourself go a little and try something new. You'll be surprised what a difference it can make for you and your audience.

 ## 7. ADD THE SEVEN Cs TO YOUR PRESENTATION

Commitment: The best speakers are committed to what they are saying. They communicate an emotion to their audience that is infectious.

Creativity: Granted, some of the topics which you may be asked to discuss will not seem very interesting. The challenge becomes how to bring them to life for your listeners. If you are talking about a new health plan for employees, you can begin with a story from your own life which personalizes the plan for your listeners. While inventory control could be a deadly subject, it becomes far more appealing if you can somehow involve your audience. Perhaps several of your listeners can offer ideas to improve the current control system. This will drive home your points by getting them more involved.

Clarity: This may be the most important asset of good speakers. They present their main ideas clearly, leaving no doubt about what they are trying to communicate. Effective speakers avoid the use of jargon and acronyms. They explain even the most difficult concepts lucidly. Finally, successful speakers solicit feedback from their audience to ensure that they completely understand every essential piece of information.

Coherence: All of the ideas flow together to form a logical pattern and a solid structure. There are no inconsistencies in the information, no material that does not belong in the presentation, and nothing to distract the audience.

Conciseness: It is an art to make your point with a minimum of words that carry a maximum of impact. This should be one of your primary goals whenever you develop a presentation and deliver it.

Correctness: All the information which a speaker presents should be carefully checked to verify its accuracy. While mistakes are always possible, remember that any serious errors will undermine your believability.

Credibility: Aristotle described the manner in which we communicate in "On Rhetoric." He stated that credibility was the most important part of the process and without it nothing else mattered. Think about people you have seen delivering a presentation and who had no credibility in your eyes. Isn't it almost impossible to believe anything they said? But with great credibility your message comes across in such a way that your listeners will respond in a more active and positive manner to whatever you are saying to them.

8. STUDY THE SKILLS OF SUCCESSFUL SPEAKERS

One of the best ways to improve your communication skills is to listen to good speakers and determine what makes them effective.

The next time you go to a presentation, whether at work, at your church, or in your community, watch and listen carefully to the speaker, and ask yourself a series of questions. By evaluating their performance, as either good or bad, you can learn things about yourself that will make you a better speaker.

Answer the following list of questions to assist in your evaluations:

Questions
& Answers

1. Does the speaker present information clearly?
    _____

2. Does the speaker use interesting anecdotes and memorable phrases to bring ideas to life for the listeners?
    _____

3. Does the presenter infuse the delivery with an infectious level of feeling?
    _____

4. Is the speaker committed to what he is saying?
    _____

5. Does the opening and closing of the presentation capture the attention of the audience?
    _____

6. Does the speaker maintain eye contact with listeners?
    _____

7. Does the presenter vary pacing, volume and inflection in the delivery?_____

8. Do the speaker's gestures support his ideas?
    _____

9. Are the visual aids clear, simple and powerful?
    _____

10. Does the speaker avoid reading or memorizing the presentation?
    _____

11. During the presentation, does the speaker involve the audience by building a dialogue with them?
    _____

12. If there is a Q&A session after the presentation, does the speaker handle it effectively?
    _____

13. Rate the overall impact of the presentation: Excellent. Good. Fair. Poor. _____

Conclusion ————————————————

Consider eight key points as you think about your next talk:

- *Understand the purpose of your presentation*
- *Make it memorable and you will be remembered*
- *Accentuate your assets: verbal, vocal and visual skills*
- *Be prepared to work hard at becoming a better speaker*
- *Focus on the benefits of good speaking for yourself and your audience*
- *Let yourself go and try something different*
- *Add the seven Cs: commitment, creativity, clarity, coherence, conciseness, correctness and credibility*
- *Study the skills of successful speakers*

CHAPTER TWO

AT THE STARTING GUN

Highlights

- *Organize your talk around a central message*
- *Make your message meaningful to the audience*
- *Conduct a listener analysis*

Several years ago, I was working with a group of MBA candidates who were completing a summer internship program at a major manufacturing company. As their final assignment, they were expected to make a report on their experiences over the preceding weeks to a team of the firm's senior executives.

"What are you going to tell them?" I asked.

"We'll just explain what we did here all summer," one of them said confidently. The others nodded their agreement.

"But what point will you try to make?" I wanted to know.

"Point?" one of them asked, looking a little confused.

13

"If you're going to present all of this information," I continued, "and you don't want to bore your listeners, it should be organized around some idea that's important to them."

Suddenly all eyes were looking down at the floor. No one wanted to speak.

Finally, a young woman raised her hand. "You mean, we need a theme?" she offered.

"Yes," I told her. "What did you learn and how will it benefit the company?"

 SENDING A MESSAGE

How many times have you sat through a presentation at a business meeting, listening to a barrage of facts and figures, while all the time wondering to yourself: "What is the speaker's main point? What is he trying to tell me?" If no answer readily emerges, you probably find yourself rapidly losing interest and drifting into listener's lethargy, doodling on your notepad, daydreaming about somewhere else you would rather be spending your time, and perhaps even closing your eyes and briefly falling asleep.

One way to prevent listener's lethargy from descending on an audience during your next talk, is to organize your information around a clear theme. Then your listeners will know why you are speaking to them, which increases the chance they will pay attention. This theme is your central message.

When you think about it, developing a presentation is much like writing a report — organizing material, communicating it clearly, etc. In their book *How to Write*, Herbert and Jill Meyer define the theme or central message this way: "The theme captures in just a few words or sentences...what it is you want to say about the subject at hand. Thus, it is not the same as the subject itself. It is more like the explanation of the subject. It answers the question: Well, what about it?"

That is the question your listeners are asking. But many speakers never seem to address it. As one of our students explained: "People feel they have to stand up and say something, but they don't know exactly what to say. They don't have a message." Instead, they often expect their audience to draw some main idea from everything that has been said. They may not come to the right conclusion so you must provide it for them.

Some of them are barely paying attention. Others soon drift away unless you explain the theme of your talk almost as soon as you begin speaking. But it will sound condescending, students often say to us, to actually tell the audience your central message. Will this insult their intelligence? No! The worst your audience might think is that you have been too clear. And no group of listeners ever criticizes a speaker for that problem.

> *"If you cannot express in a sentence or two what it is you intend to get across, then it is not focused well enough."*
>
> *— Charles Osgood*
> *Author and TV Commentator*

The central message is like the saying you find inside a fortune cookie — a concise statement that should be easy to remember. Sometimes it can be difficult to think about a presentation in these terms, especially if you are someone who has a hard time coming to the point. Consider your listeners, for a moment. Each day they absorb large quantities of information, much of which is promptly forgotten. But you can be the exception.

This means organizing your material around a single idea. Align the information much the way a magnet aligns a collection of iron filings, so that everything is pointing in the same direction and your listeners cannot possibly miss the message.

To accomplish this task, start with the topic and narrow it until you have defined your central message.   Usually it should be stated to your audience in terms of what you want to accomplish: to inform...to persuade...to explain...to initiate action. Here are several examples:

TOPIC	CENTRAL MESSAGE
1. A talk about recent activities in your department at the annual sales meeting.	"I will explain how my office served the sales representatives more effectively in the past year."
2. A discussion of the pension benefits at the orientation meeting for new employees.	"I want to inform you of special features that make our pension program particularly valuable."
3. A description of a new real estate investment program at a meeting of the executive board.	"I want you to agree to let me pursue the real estate investment program, by showing you its advantages."
4. A discussion of a new physical fitness program at an employee meeting.	"I'd like to enroll you in our new physical fitness program by pointing out how it can improve your health."

It is a good idea to state the central message near the beginning of your talk, so the audience knows almost immediately why you are addressing them. Think of it as a good newspaper story, with the main idea near the front and all of the details following behind it. Think of this as the pyramid structure of writing. (Fig. 1)

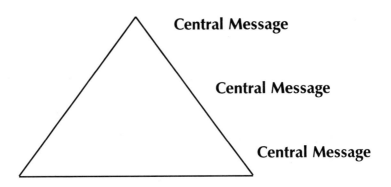

Suppose you were talking about that physical fitness program, for example, you would tell your listeners very early that a regular exercise regimen could improve their health. Then you would add details to support your message. You might repeat it again, adding some additional facts and statistics. Then you would reinforce the central message by stating it once more in the conclusion of your talk, before asking the employees to enroll in the program.

 ## SO WHAT?

Today meetings will take place in organizations across America. Indeed, some executives report that they spend up to twenty-three hours each week in formal meetings. If you must make a presentation in one of them and do not want to lose your audience, you better make sure that your central message has some relevance to them. This is the meaning of the message.

When you are preparing a talk, you should always be asking yourself: How can I appeal to the interests of my audience? What will be really meaningful to them? Recently a large printing company embarked on a re-engineering program. Management knew that once this initiative was announced, employees would be afraid of losing their jobs. So the CEO immediately assured everyone that re-engineering did not mean downsizing. Instead, he pointed out that it was designed to make their jobs easier, enabling them to reduce needless steps in their operations, cut down on re-work, and improving overall efficiency. He could have pitched re-engineering as something that would improve returns on an investment and benefit stockholders. But this would not have been especially relevant to the employees. He presented his message in a way that would have the most meaning for them.

Another way to think about the relevance of your message is the "so what" test. Will my audience come away wondering why they have been listening to me — asking so what? Will they understand how my presentation impacts them? You should be able to answer this question by writing out the meaning of your message in a brief sentence or two, otherwise your speech may not be as relevant to your audience as they would like.

CENTRAL MESSAGE   MEANING OF THE MESSAGE

1. "I want to explain why   This will impact your bonus
   sales in the division were   payment for the year.
   down by 15%."

2. "I am informing you that   Non-compliance can result in
   the company is revamping   heavy fines.
   its product safety program
   to comply with federal laws."

3. "I want you to agree to my   The new facility will expedite
   proposal to fund a new   the R&D process bringing new
   laboratory facility."   products to market sooner and
                                    increasing sales.

Like the central message, its meaning to your listeners should be placed near the beginning of your talk, that is, at the top of the pyramid. It is another way to assure that your listeners sit up and take notice of what you are saying to them. Throughout the talk, you should also reiterate the meaning of the message, so your listeners never lose sight of it. (Fig. 2)

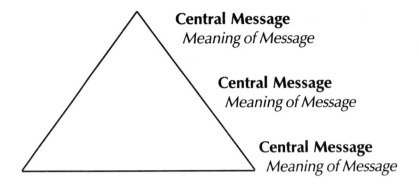

Central Message
Meaning of Message

Central Message
Meaning of Message

Central Message
Meaning of Message

This approach may sound repetitive and didactic until you begin looking at presentations from the listener's viewpoint. You may know where you are taking an audience as you lead them through a forest of information. But they don't. They need signposts and constant encouragement or they may lose their way and lose interest. Stating your central message and the meaning of your message, then repeating them periodically, help to keep listeners on the same trail that you are traveling. As you begin preparing for your next presentation, complete the planning exercise on the following page.

PLANNING EXERCISE

PRESENTATION #1

Topic:

_____

_____

Central Message:

_____

_____

_____

Meaning of the Message:

_____

_____

_____

PRESENTATION #2

Topic:

_____

_____

Central Message:

_____

_____

_____

Meaning of the Message:

_____

_____

_____

 **AN OUNCE OF PREVENTION:
A LISTENER ANALYSIS**

In American corporations, change is the order of the day, and the pace seems to be accelerating. Some employees even appear to be growing accustomed to it. "Change is an opportunity," one CEO recently told us, referring to the acquisition of his company by a larger competitor. But many others might disagree. For them, change disrupts the established routines, and it often forces employees to redefine their jobs, or even worse, creates a fear that these jobs will be eliminated. So if you have to announce a change process, make sure you know where your audience stands on the issue, namely their *attitudes*, otherwise your presentation could be a total flop. Indeed, this applies to any important speech you may be planning.

How do you find out about the attitudes of your audience? You probably work with some of your listeners, so you have already heard their opinions or, at the very least, have an idea of what they think. Most executives also have established networks of information in their organization. If you don't personally know some of your listeners, you may be acquainted with someone else who does. This is the time to tap into your network and discover what you can before that exciting day when it's time to deliver your presentation.

Do the listeners share your vision of change? Are they afraid of being fired if the change occurs or are their jobs secure? Will they be forced to give up some of their turf or will they gain some? Will they need to learn new skills or do they already possess the necessary know-how to succeed in a new environment? These are only a few of the questions you must ask yourself to determine the attitudes of your audience. More than likely, their attitudes will not be uniform. And you should probably focus your attention on those with the greatest resistance to change. This will enable you to shape your central message and the meaning of your message in a way that is most effective.

Another question you must ask yourself is how much knowledge your audience already possesses about the topic. If they have been informed about various aspects of the change process, you do not want to repeat information needlessly. This will not only bore your audience, but you also run the risk of sounding very patronizing, which will alienate them. However, what if your listeners' knowledge varies, ranging from uninformed employees to those who are fully briefed on the subject? If you speak over the heads of the former, you risk losing their support, while the latter may find it tedious to go back over ground that they have already covered. Perhaps the best you can do is proceed to communicate the information in a clear and succinct manner so that everyone can understand.

It is not only important to ask yourself how much an audience needs to know, but what they want to know. We talked earlier about making the information relevant to your audience. Clearly, a group of shareholders will want to know something different about the firm's impending change process than the employees in the manufacturing area. Once again, your listener analysis will help you to determine what is most meaningful to them.

Finally, it is very useful to understand the positions that your listeners hold within the organization. For example, top executives generally view the world differently from first line supervisors. And your approach will be partially determined by the perspectives of your audience. If the senior management team recognizes the importance of targeting new markets, there is no need to re-emphasize this point with them. However, supervisors in customer service may not have this perspective, so you will need to enlighten them.

LISTENER ANALYSIS

Indicate the number of listeners who fall at each point on the continuum.

ATTITUDES OF THE AUDIENCE

Supportive   Indifferent   Negative
_____

KNOWLEDGE OF AUDIENCE

Expert   Some Knowledge   Uninformed
_____

POSITIONS OF AUDIENCE

Top Executives   Managers   Supervisors   Employees
_____

PLANNING YOUR PRESENTATION

"If only I had a little more time to get ready." How often have you said this to yourself after you have given a presentation? Your opening might have been more powerful or your delivery more professional or your visual aids more creative if you only left yourself some extra time to prepare them.

Of course, every presentation can stand some improvement. And there is nothing easier than Monday morning quarterbacking. Yet successful presentations, like winning football teams, are the ones that are well prepared. The key to adequate preparation is effective time management.

Time can be a valuable resource if you use it wisely. But how many of us do? It is so much easier to put off preparing for a presentation until the last minute, to assume that you can get it done in just a few hours, only to find out that it is not enough time to do the job.

Several years ago a client called Focus Communications to ask for help in preparing a presentation designed to obtain adequate funding for his department. The entire future of his employees hinged on a talk he was delivering to the executive committee. Yet he had waited until two days before the meeting to begin his preparation. This simply was not a sufficient amount of time.

When it comes to presentations, many of us are procrastinators. It is very easy to put off something, especially if you feel the least bit apprehensive about doing it. This may be exactly how you approach the prospect of giving a talk. Perhaps the deadline seems so far in the future that you simply put it on the back burner. More pressing problems intervene that require your immediate attention. The presentation is almost forgotten until one day when you turn over the next page on your calendar and realize that the deadline is almost here. Panic grips you. You race around at the very last minute trying to get ready. Unfortunately, the quality of your presentation usually suffers and, with it, your reputation as a successful communicator.

Preparing for a presentation, like any other important project, requires effective time management (that is, if you want to do it right). First, look at the tasks to be accomplished in your preparation. Second, plan carefully. Allot enough time to adequately complete every task. Third, schedule these tasks. Set aside certain periods of time each week to complete all the elements of your presentation.

What are these elements? We have already covered three of them: Defining your central message, shaping the meaning of that message, and conducting a listener analysis. You can probably determine how much time will be necessary to accomplish them.

Your other tasks will include the following: gathering ideas for your presentation, collecting information to support them, writing an outline, developing your talk, creating visual aids, and rehearsing your delivery.

How much time will you need to complete each one of them? Your own experience is the best guide. You can base your estimates on previous speeches or informal talks that you have prepared. Once you have allotted what seems to be a sufficient amount of time for each task, then add a little more. Do not forget Murphy's Law of Presentations.

Every schedule should be written down so you can refer to it easily and remind yourself of what needs to be accomplished and when it has to be done. You do not have to block out large amounts of time to work on a particular task. Often, two or three hours may not be available to you. Instead, try to set aside 15 minutes or 30 minutes a day. You will be surprised at how much you can accomplish and what a significant effect it will have on your presentation.

Use the following Presentation Planner to do your scheduling:

PRESENTATION PLANNER

Week #	Planned	Accomplished
Monday		
Tuesday		
Wednesday		
Thursday		
Friday		
Weekend		

Conclusion

1. Every successful presentation has a central message or theme which captures, in just a few words, what you want to say about the subject at hand.

2. The central message should have meaning or relevance to your listeners if you want them to pay attention to your talk.

3. By conducting a listener analysis you can determine the attitudes of the audience toward your central message and deliver it as effectively as possible.

4. Preparing for a presentation, like any other important project, requires effective time management.

CHAPTER THREE

OUT OF THE STARTING BLOCKS

Highlights

- *Ideas are the basis of successful presentations*
- *Include ideas that support your central message*
- *Anecdotes and examples bring a talk to life*

Recently, we asked one of the students in a Focus Communications seminar if he had heard any good speeches at his company lately.

"No," he told us. "The most inspiring talk I have listened to was given by someone at my church who was speaking about community action."

"What made it so memorable?" we wanted to know.

"He had obviously thought a lot about what he wanted to say — the main message was clear. It was also delivered with a great deal of energy. And it included his own personal experiences. This made it very moving."

Perhaps the most important question you should ask yourself whenever you develop a presentation is this: How can I hold the attention
of my audience? This should guide every phase of your preparation
— from the information you gather to selecting the best nuggets to
present to your listeners, from constructing a logical flow of ideas
to perfecting your delivery. You want to engage their attention as
you speak. If you lose your audience, you might just as well stop
speaking because they will not be listening anyway. In fact, many
of our students comment on how difficult it is for them to pay attention during business meetings. This often occurs because the speaker
does not communicate a message clearly. Thus, if you can concentrate on your listeners and focus your message effectively, you will
be much more successful.

Too many speakers fall back on that handy rationalization: "I have a
dull topic, so how do you expect me to make it interesting?" Your
challenge is to take the driest information and figure out how to
breathe life into it for your audience. Otherwise you will probably
be squandering your energies and wasting their time. If you cannot
make your presentation interesting for them, it may be much more
productive to send a memo and let your colleagues read it in their
offices, thus saving them time.

 ## IT BEGINS WITH BRAINSTORMING

Ideas are the stuff of which every talk is born. These are the building blocks of a successful presentation. And the more of them you
can collect, the better.

Of course, this doesn't mean that you'll actually use everything that
you gather. Indeed, you should not or you will risk burying your
listeners under a blizzard of information that will only overwhelm
them. But the more you gather, the more you have to select from,

and the better will be the kernels of information which you can finally present to your audience.

Suppose the safety record has been declining at several of the manufacturing facilities which your company operates. You must present a proposal to the executive committee designed to deal with this problem and improve safety. How do you begin?

One of the best approaches is brainstorming. While you are taking a shower, commuting to work, or sitting at lunch, an idea may pop into your head and you should try to jot it down as soon as possible.

Use a Brainstorming Board. This is a central location where you can collect all of your ideas. Write them down on napkins or the backs of business cards as you think of them, but then transfer all of your thoughts to one place — the Brainstorming Board. This can be a special file in your computer, or a bulletin board, or even a legal pad that is dedicated to the preparation for your talk. It takes only a few minutes each day to record information on the Brainstorming Board, but when you get ready to begin organizing your speech, you will find it was time exceedingly well spent because much of the information you need will be conveniently located and easy to access.

The primary goal of brainstorming is to collect as many ideas as possible. Quantity is the watchword, not quality. You can evaluate the significance of the ideas and decide whether or not to keep them in your talk later. At this point, it is only important to list ideas — plenty of them — so you will have plenty to choose from when you develop your presentation.

Suppose you start with the task of answering the following question: *How do we improve the plants' safety record?* Your list might look like the following.

BRAINSTORMING BOARD

current employee attitudes
safety vs. productivity
management emphasis on safety
number of days lost at each plant
plant accident records
successful program at
    Centerville plant
testimonials by Centerville employees
"safety awareness" days
community attitudes toward safety
    at our plants
number of employee days lost
effect of safety on "bottom line"

role of safety committees in
    new effort
safety poster campaign
articles in plant newsletters
contests among work teams
how employees' families value
    safety
speeches by plant managers
special announcements
    by CEO
number of first aid cases
community involvement
    programs

After you have gathered a list of ideas, you can go back later and determine the ones that are most relevant to your listeners. Your selection criteria should be the central message and the meaning of that message. Only the ideas that best support both of them should remain. The rest should be eliminated. If your central message is that the company needs to begin a new safety campaign and you want to persuade the executive committee to undertake the initiative that you are proposing, you must ask yourself which ideas will be most persuasive. You also need to keep your listeners in mind. In this case, you are speaking to top management so your words must convince them. But your proposals will eventually be aimed at rank and file employees —so the executive committee must be assured that your ideas will also work with the people on the front lines, too. Indeed, you may want to have a separate list of ideas for each audience. Their needs and interests may be very different.

One set of ideas for your presentation may be relevant to an executive group. However, another group may be totally uninterested in these ideas and react much more positively to a different set of ideas affecting them. Delivering your presentation to different audiences requires you to custom-tailor it to each group. This is not a very time consuming process. Your listener analysis should reveal the needs and interests of your audience and determine which ideas will have the greatest impact on them.

Using this criteria, you can now review the ideas on your Brainstorming Board. Put a (+) next to the ones you want to keep and cross out the rest.

> *" 'Really, now you ask me,' said Alice,*
> *very much confused. 'I don't think—'*
> *'Then you shouldn't talk,' said the Hatter."*
> — *Lewis Carroll,* **Alice in Wonderland**

 LEAD BY EXAMPLE

If the central message and the meaning of the message form the backbone of your presentation, and if the ideas on your Brainstorming Board comprise the skeleton, then information is the flesh and blood that gives your talk substance. In his book, *The Leadership Factor*, John Kotter of Harvard University points out that leaders at every level of an organization must be skilled in synthesizing vast quantities of data and putting new patterns on it so they can create a meaningful agenda to communicate to other people. This is your role as a speaker — to organize information around a central message so your listeners can make sense of what you are trying to tell them. Share your perceptions, your thoughts, your agenda. The memorable speaker, just like the successful leader, is the one who does it best.

A significant amount of the information you collect for any talk will consist of facts and statistics designed to add muscle to those ideas that make up the skeleton we just mentioned. But if you stop here, you have not really done your job very well. Presentations that only contain facts and statistics can become quite dull. Anecdotes, examples, personal experiences, unusual tidbits of information — these are the special elements that will make your speech unforgettable, at least as far as your audience is concerned. After all, they are the ones you have to satisfy and persuade.

For instance, if you decide to talk about community attitudes toward your plant safety practices, what better way than to quote from a local newspaper article or present the comments you have personally received from community leaders? If you are planning to discuss safety posters, why not illustrate your point with an example from one of the plants or by talking about successful poster campaigns used by companies considered to be the best in your industry? If you are discussing the role of safety committees, anecdotes gleaned from outstanding committees in your company can add human interest and minimize the impersonal nature of facts and statistics.

Suppose you are the marketing vice president of a chain of toy stores who is trying to make a persuasive case for developing a mail order catalog as a way of bringing shopping services directly to the customer instead of the other way around. In addition to all of the facts and figures regarding costs and a detailed analysis of your competition, you could also add anecdotes. Select the best ones you have collected from friends who already enjoy the convenience of buying toys through the mail, or borrow from the personal experiences of your children who are avid catalog shoppers. These examples help make the information you are presenting more concrete, more real. Properly placed throughout a presentation, they can also add variety to your repertoire — and there is nothing better than variety to keep your audience from falling asleep.

To test this advice, the next time you have to present a substantial quantity of statistical information, follow it with the words, "Now let me tell you a story." Watch the way your audience reacts. They hunger for animated tales to enliven the material and data being presented to them.

While some of these stories may already lie at your fingertips, finding the others will probably take some digging. This process can eat up a considerable number of hours in your busy schedule, which is one of the reasons we urged you in the previous chapter to set aside sufficient time for presentation planning and preparation. Books, articles, reports, conversations with colleagues — each can be a valuable source of examples and quotable quotes. They also serve as sources of the facts and statistics that you need to buttress your ideas.

It is also helpful to keep a file of this information. You may want to file it together with your Brainstorming Board. Then, as you start to develop your talk, you can summarize the examples and anecdotes, and write down the quotes under the appropriate ideas that you have decided to present. This material should appear along with any of the hard data you have collected. Next to each entry, you might also list its source — article, report, etc., in case you need to refer back to it.

IDEAS AND INFORMATION

IDEA _____

      QUOTE _____

_____

_____

         SOURCE _____

    EXAMPLE _____

_____

_____

_____

         SOURCE _____

*ANECDOTE*_____

_____

_____

_____

                    SOURCE _____

          *STATISTICS*_____

_____

_____

_____

                    SOURCE _____

          FACTS _____

_____

_____

_____

                    SOURCE _____

EVALUATING YOUR PROGRESS

The previous exercise should enable you to look at the information
you have already gathered, see where it is concentrated and decide
in what areas you still need more. Some ideas may have little or no
supporting data, so you must collect it. Perhaps many ideas are top
heavy with factual support, but lack any interesting examples. These
may be buried somewhere in your file, or finding them may require
a little additional research.

Developing a talk is somewhat like decorating the inside of a house.
Think of each room as a main idea and the information that supports
it as the furniture, wallpaper, carpets, lighting fixtures, draperies,
paint and other accessories.

Designing each room of the house should present a challenge to your creativity. If every room is painted the same color or contains identical furniture, your home will appear monotonous. A presentation suffers from a similar problem when every idea is introduced and then supported in the same way — that is, always by a fact or always with an example drawn from the pages of your favorite business magazine. Ideas are like rooms: they need a splash of one color here, another color there, as well as different types of furniture, lighting and draperies to add interest and zest for everyone.

As you survey your ideas and supporting information, an overview of the presentation will gradually come into focus. You will spot the holes, recognize where an appropriate story might be necessary to illustrate your point, decide that the quotation you have found really does not seem to fit and you will need another one. As you conduct this process, always try to put yourself into the chairs of your listeners: What will they want to hear? How can I make my ideas as clear as possible for them? What will interest them? What will they remember?

The following material is an excerpt from a business presentation that exemplifies some of the concepts we have just discussed. You will notice how main ideas are introduced and supported in a variety of ways to make them meaningful to the audience.

PRESENTATION EXCERPT

Reference to Quote   It was the anthropoligist Margaret Mead who once said that change is occurring so rapidly that middle-aged adults won't be able to keep up with it. Our children will be teaching us how to do things.

Example   This has already happened to some of us in the computer field. Indeed, I know a financial services firm whose MIS department only wanted to hire people under 30. It may sound like age discrimnation. But they seem to believe that these are the only people who can really keep up with changes in the computer field.

I do not agree. But I also know that dealing with the ever accelerating rate of change and mastering it is the greatest challenge facing all of us as we approach the 21st century.

Central Message

Today, I would like to talk with you about the changes affecting our business, how they have already impacted us, and how we will continue to deal with them in the future.

Meaning of the Message

Organizations who, for whatever reason, find themselves incapable of adjusting to the pace of change can easily find themselves falling behind the competition...losing market share...and eventually becoming irrelevant to their customers.

Idea

This was the problem that our bank faced in the early 1990s. We may have had the world's best loan officers and tellers, but we did not have the marketing expertise necessary to detect the profound changes occurring in the marketplace. And right under our noses, the competition began to whittle away at our customer base.

Personal Anecdote

I will never forget walking into a supermarket and seeing the customers doing their banking at a new branch opened by one of our competitors. They had brought their services to the customer instead of the other way around.

Idea

That should have been us, but it wasn't. And I realized we had to begin refocusing our efforts in the future, or risk falling even further behind our competition.

Statistic   What that meant was some painful readjustments. As you know, we have downsized our workforce by 25 percent and reduced the layers of management hierarchy within our organization from seven to three. Frankly, this was a very difficult experience for everyone. But it was a necessary step in redirecting our entire operation.

Idea   What was the nature of that redirection? In a single word...the customer. We wanted to become a customer-driven company.

Example   Now, there is nothing new or unique about this. The world's best companies have always been focused on the customer. Hewlett-Packard, the electronics giant, for example, is constantly talking to customers and asking them what they like...and, yes, do not like...about their products. Then HP uses this information to make improvements.

Idea   Here at the bank we have become more customer-focused, too. For example, we are spending more time with our business customers, especially people running small businesses. This enables us to go more in-depth so we can better understand their problems and help them find workable solutions. Our customers are dealing with the same kinds of market demands that we are, and they value the experience and expertise we have to offer them.

Anecdote/Quote   Just recently, one of our loan officers received this note from a customer. It says, in part: "Thanks for explaining everything so thoroughly. It makes quite a difference to know that you really do care what happens to us — and that it is more than just protecting the bank's investment."

How many banks do you know that seem more interested in protecting their assets than serving the customer? Apparently, they seem to have forgotten where their assets came from.

Idea

But our managers are not forgetting. And we are recognizing them for their efforts.

Example

The employee who received the note I just mentioned was Carol Broder and she was singled out at our monthly management meeting with a special award. She is not the first, nor will she be the last.

Idea

Of course, recognition is only part of our effort aimed at creating a culture dedicated to serving the customer. It also requires extensive training. So we have been training employees at all levels of the organization in various critical skills that are essential pre-requisites to becoming more customer-focused.

Example

Training lies at the foundation of every successful organization. Take Federal Express, for example. They are known throughout their industry as a company whose employees have been highly trained to satisfy the customer.

Or Motorola, where employees attend more hours of training annually than almost any other company in America. Both of them are also winners of the prestigious Baldrige Award for quality.

Idea

An important result of all this training is employee empowerment. We have empowered employees to take on more responsibility...we have entrusted them to make more decisions...and we can hold them more accountable because they are better trained.

Personal
Anecdote
This has not only improved our service to the customers but the morale of our employees. At one of my regular breakfasts that I hold throughout the year with employees in each department, one of them stood up and said: "I wish you had done this five years ago. It has improved my whole job."

Now let me take a few moments to speak about the future.....

Conclusion

1. Brainstorming helps you collect ideas for your presentation. Quantity is the watchword, not quality.

2. Select only those ideas that support your central message and the meaning of your message.

3. Facts and statistics add muscle to your presentation.

4. Anecdotes, examples and personal experiences bring your presentation to life.

5. Keep a file of interesting anecdotes, etc., to help you develop your next talk.

CHAPTER FOUR

LEAPING THE HURDLES

Highlights

- *A tightly organized talk will be more meaningful to listeners*
- *Use one of several organizing patterns for your presentation*
- *Develop an outline for your talk*

"I have trouble putting everything I need to say into a 20-minute talk," one executive said.

"I'm just terrible at public speaking," another manager admitted. "I cannot remember anything. It just blows me away."

"The toughest presentation I had to give occured when my manager asked me to speak to a group of people touring our plant," a supervisor explained, "I was very nervous until I came up to speed and figured out how to organize the talk."

How to organize your material may be one of the most difficult issues facing anyone who must deliver a presentation. All of us have heard those speakers who were not well organized — they seem to meander around forever hunting for their main points. By contrast,

41

a clear, tight organizational structure can enable you to deliver a talk that does not run overtime, will help you remember what you want to say, and make the talk meaningful to your audience.

If you have ever tried to organize a presentation, you know that the same questions keep coming up over and over again: What idea do I present first? How many ideas should I try to cover? Which ones do I keep in...and leave out?

For starters, every idea should relate to your central message, or it does not belong in the presentation. The central message forms the cornerstone of your entire talk and each idea should build on it. What's more, every anecdote, example or quote should be connected to one of your main ideas. Otherwise, it will seem out of place in the presentation. That is where organization begins...but it is not the only thing you can do.

There are also several time-tested patterns of presenting material that can give your talk a tight, solid structure. These patterns can help you decide which idea to present first, what comes next, and how many ideas to include. Although every talk, by no means, lends itself to one of these patterns or even a combination of them; many do. For the speaker, a basic organizing pattern can provide the structure for a presentation outline. The process of developing an outline is a critically important step that should precede the delivery of any presentation. An outline is one of the best ways to assure yourself that all the important ideas have not only been included in your speech, but that they also flow logically together in a way that your listeners can easily understand.

 TYPES OF ORGANIZING PATTERNS

Delivering a talk is somewhat like painting a picture. An artist fills the canvas with images that are organized according to a specific pattern. A landscape painter, for example, might depict a pleasant pastoral scene with cows in the foreground, a barn and a house behind them, and gently rolling hills in the background. Or a still-life painting might begin with a bunch of cherries on the left side of a table, a blue and white bowl in the middle and several yellow squash on the right to provide balance. Each of these pictures is organized in a pattern that would be recognizable to an audience, which makes them easier to comprehend.

In public speaking, if you can organize the material according to a model that is familiar to your listeners, it makes the information you present much easier for them to absorb, and the connections between your ideas much more readily recognizable. The organizing structure gives unity to the material, just the way a good landscape painting possesses unity. Several effective organizing patterns include: chronology, location, hierarchical, proposal-benefits, and key points.

CHRONOLOGY:

"Four score and seven years ago..." begins the most famous speech ever written by an American. Abraham Lincoln opened the Gettysburg Address by talking about his nation's past. And he wrote, it was "conceived in liberty" by the Declaration of Independence, and "dedicated to the proposition that all men are created equal." From there, Lincoln went on to a brief discussion of the present -- the great Civil War currently engulfing the nation and the battle fought between the Union and Confederate soldiers at Gettysburg only a few months earlier. Finally, Lincoln took his listeners into the future, prophesying that "these dead shall not have died in vain" and that there would be "a new birth of freedom" in the United States.

Chronological patterns in talks follow a sequence of time order: yesterday, today and tomorrow; 1900, 1950, 2000. It is one of the most recognizable patterns for most listeners. After all, our lives progress according to this pattern; and many types of books, such as history and biography, are presented in this way. The talks delivered at a retirement dinner frequently utilize a chronological pattern: the speaker begins by recalling the retiree's first days with the organization and ends with the latest accomplishments.

A speaker might also use a chronological approach to present a glowing report on his department's record of steady improvement: "Two years ago, our sales office was near the middle of the pack in terms of units sold. Last year we were number three and this year we have become number one in the company."

A variation of the historical chronology is what is sometimes called "the steps in a process." These must follow a certain order for the process to be successful, and, therefore, they are usually presented as Step 1...Step 2...Step 3...etc. or as Phase 1, 2, 3, etc.

Presentation Organizing Plan*

Here is a sample usage of the chronological approach.

Central Message: We need to increase employee initiative in our department to make it more productive.

Step 1: Survey employees and find out what factors are preventing them from taking more initiative.

Step 2: Design a training program to deal with these issues. This can be done by human resources department or by an outside consulting firm.

Step 3: Field test the program, make any necessary changes and train everyone in the department.

Step 4: Require periodic progress reports by participants; and acknowledge their accomplishments with various awards and recognition ceremonies.

* For purposes of illustration, this plan and those that follow have been kept brief. Much more information can be added, including anecdotes, quotes, etc. related to each main idea.

The most effective presentations of this type include only a few steps — too many, and the audience begins to lose track of them, which undercuts the entire impact of the talk. A speaker who is presenting the 17 Steps to Quality Improvement, for example, is almost guaranteed his audience will lose interest and start daydreaming about something else long before he reaches the end.

A chronological approach to organizing information is often used to train new employees on various types of procedures. These might include the step by step approach to processing a customer's order or operating a piece of equipment on the manufacturing floor.

Sometimes a speaker may use a chronological organization pattern, but decide to present the chronology out of order. An example might be a status or progress report, such as the following:

Presentation Organizing Plan

Central Message: Our fund-raising effort has met with mixed success this year.

Current Year: After making every effort, we have failed to meet our fund raising targets. Small donors are hesitant to give money because they are nervous about losing their jobs due to corporate downsizings.

Previous Year: We exceeded our targets because of all the excitement about kicking off the fund raising campaign. Also, we received money from our traditionally large donors.

Next Year: We expect to improve our performance due to a new publicity campaign and stronger efforts to tap new sources of donations.

So far, this chapter has been describing presentations that primarily convey information or explain a procedure to an audience. But the chronological approach can also be utilized to inspire your listeners and persuade them to take action. For example, you can try to build on your audience's past performance and challenge them to do even more in the future. This is called the "good...better...best" speech.

Presentation Organization Plan

Central Message: We must work harder to beat the competition.

Five years ago: They said our company was finished in the widget business, but you showed them that we could survive.

Two years ago: The competition said that their new widget would out-perform ours. But we came up with something even better.

Today: Everyone is telling us that we cannot compete in international markets. But we will create a new widget that will be the best in the world.

This type of organization plan provides a skeleton for your presentation — that is, it gives you a model for how to sequence your ideas. Then, under each idea, you can add supporting information, as we've explained earlier.

Practice Exercise
Practice the chronolgical plan with the following examples:

1. A talk at a testimonial dinner for a colleague in your department.

_____

_____

_____

_____

_____

_____

_____

2. A status report on the development of a new product.

_____

_____

_____

_____

_____

_____

_____

3. A humorous talk on the process for making an automobile insurance claim.

_____

_____

_____

_____

_____

_____

LOCATION:

When an artist paints a landscape, the canvas is organized spatially by the location of the objects — placing some in the foreground and others in the background, some on the left side of the canvas, others in the center, and still others on the right. If you were to talk to an audience about the subject matter of picture-painting, you might organize your presentation much like the painting itself, that is, according to the location of the objects in it. Many types of talks rely on this method of arranging information to make the material easier for an audience to understand.

Suppose, for example, you were presenting a talk on re-organizing the manufacturing operation to improve work flow on the factory floor. You might organize the presentation according to the new location of each work center, beginning at one end of the factory and continuing to the other end. In addition, you would probably rely on visual aids to show your audience the spatial location of each manufacturing process.

Speakers use a spatial pattern of organization in presenting other types of material, as well. For example, a top level manager might review the company's sales figures for the past year, territory by territory — Southeast, Midwest, Northwest, etc. Or one of the speakers at a printing firm's executive conference might talk about overall productivity in terms of the figures for each plant location (Nashville, St. Louis, etc.), explaining why some plants were more successful than others. Let us review the following example:

Presentation Organizing Plan

Central Message: We have a unique opportunity to expand our international sales of Bow Wow Dog Products.

Latin America: Bow Wow has enormous name recognition, so we can add some new products to our already successful line.

Eastern Europe: This is an expanding market. There is no competition for our Bow Wow gourmet dog treats or our complete line of dog sweaters.

Pacific Rim: We propose to open new sales offices and increase advertising of our canine TV dinners and bedtime snacks. This will enable us to expand market share in the area.

Practice Exercise

Practice the location pattern of organization with the following examples.

1. A talk that reviews company-wide safety programs in each manufacturing location.

_____

_____

_____

_____

_____

2. A brief tour of your plant.

_____

_____

_____

_____

_____

3. A proposal for expanding sales of your company's products in several regional markets.

_____

_____

_____

_____

_____

HIERARCHICAL:

For years, management consultants have been expounding on the subject of flattening corporate hierarchies. While companies may have shed numerous layers of management, some form of hierarchy will no doubt always exist — if only because it seems to be the natural order of things, whether it is a business, a school, the government, or even a family unit. A hierarchical pattern is also a natural way to organize some presentations. Suppose, for example, a large corporation is forced to downsize and announces the sever-

ance packages for employees who are being laid off. The presentation might discuss typical financial packages for top managers, mid-
level bosses and clerical workers.

Sometimes a hierarchical presentation can begin at the bottom of
the pyramid and work its way up. It may depend on the audience.
For instance, a speaker might be talking to a group of aircraft workers about the importance of lifetime learning as a way of remaining
current with technological changes in their industry. Given the
makeup of his audience, he might start with what they can do to
constantly revitalize their skills. Then, to reassure them that they
are not the only ones being asked to make this commitment, he might
talk about efforts being made at higher levels of the organization —
by managers, for example, and their superiors.

Presentation Organizing Plan

Central Message: To respond to rapid changes in the marketplace, we need leadership at every level of our
organization.

CEO: It is essential for this leader to present a vision that
guides the organization. He must exemplify the values of
the corporate culture, understand the overall direction of
our industry, and create the internal corporate environment
we need to remain competitive.

Managers: They play critical roles in carrying out the vision.
They act as mentors for subordinates, coaches for work teams,
effective communicators.

Employees: They must be empowered to take the initiative
and make decisions. They are often closest to the problems
and have the most knowledge of how to solve them.

Sometimes the hierarchical and chronological approaches work together. For example, a speaker talking about change in the organization might begin by discussing a pilot program that was instituted in a department at one of the plants. Then he would explain that, in the second phase, the program went plant-wide. Finally, he would point out that, because of its success, the program was adopted by every plant in the company.

Practice Exercise
Practice the hierarchical pattern with the following examples:

1. A talk about efforts at the federal, state and local level to deal with a serious issue, such as crime or pollution or education.

_____
_____
_____
_____
_____

2. A plan to help a nonprofit organization raise additional funds, that involves the volunteers who work there, the paid staff, and the director.

_____
_____
_____
_____
_____
_____

3. A bottom-up program to improve product quality.

_____
_____
_____
_____

PROPOSAL-BENEFITS:

Speakers often use this pattern when they are trying to persuade an audience to adopt their recommendation or their solution to a problem. For example, you might be trying to convince your listeners that the company should consider a new procedure to handle customer complaints or a new stress reduction program to deal with employee burnout. Generally, the place to begin is by establishing the need for your proposal. For instance, you might point out that the average complaint now takes far too long to resolve, resulting in dissatisfied customers. Then you might present your solution for dealing with this problem, stressing its benefits to the organization and outlining the resources that might be necessary to implement it — including the costs, training for employees, additional staff, etc. The presentation might also propose a time line for phasing in the new program.

Presentation Organizing Plan

Central Message: We need to double the number of service technicians in our Southwestern region.

Problem: Sales have increased enormously in this area. Customers need technicians to service our machines and they complain when this service is not available within 24 hours. We risk losing customers to our competition if we do not solve this problem.

Proposal: Hire additional technicians to reduce the amount of time that customers have to wait for service. This will enable us to match the competition, whom customers tell us are much more responsive to their requests.

Resources to Implement Program: Salaries and benefits for new technicians; one month training program on our equipment.

Sometimes a problem may be fairly obvious to your listeners, so they may be readily receptive to your proposal for dealing with it. On the other hand, your audience may be filled with skeptics who require a lot of convincing before they will accept your plan. This will require some strong powers of persuasion. You may need to present the problem in stark terms — not overstating its seriousness, but at the same time leaving no doubt among your listeners that something must be done to deal with it as soon as possible. Then you can show how your proposal provides an effective solution. Try to anticipate any objections that might be raised by your listeners — such as cost, etc. — and deal with them as you present your proposal.

Practice Exercise

Practice the proposal-benefit pattern with the following examples.

1. A proposal to introduce flex-time into your department.

_____

_____

_____

_____

_____

_____

2. A talk about the need to reduce the number of company trainers and utilize the CD-ROM more extensively in employee training.

_____

_____

_____

_____

_____

_____

3. A proposal to consolidate several departments or offices.

_____

_____

_____

_____

_____

_____

_____

KEY POINTS:

One of the most common methods of organizing material for a talk is to simply define the key points you want to make about your central message and present them to your listeners.

Examples might include the essential attributes of successful leaders, or the ways to improve communication in your department, or why your organization should increase the number of internships it offers to college students. This material may not lend itself to be organized according to any of the other patterns which we discussed. Nevertheless, you can present it in the form of key bullet points: Point 1, 2, 3, etc. — which will make the information much easier for your audience to follow and remember. Here are some issues to keep in mind as you organize the information.

How many points should you present? Keep the number to a handfull. Otherwise, your audience will begin to feel overwhelmed and tune out. You will know when they have started losing interest. They will begin glancing out the windows, fidgeting in their seats, closing their eyes, looking down at their laps, or just staring at you blankly.

To avoid this problem, we suggest that you present no more than 5-7 points. For those of you who have trouble organizing material this way, you are probably saying: "But there is so much more I could say." Perhaps there is. But some of it might easily be combined with one of your existing points. The rest might be better left for some other time when your audience is fresher.

How do you determine which points to include? You must prioritize them — it is the same way you would go about setting goals for yourself or your subordinates. Approach this problem by putting yourself in the shoes of your listeners. What do they need to know? Want to know? What will have the greatest impact on them? Remember, your information should be as meaningful and relevant as possible to your listeners.

Which point should you present first? Some speakers prefer to organize their material in the order of its importance. They present their most important point first to grab the attention of their listeners and work their way down to the least important. Others do just the reverse — beginning with the least important and finish with a climax, by presenting their most significant point near the end of the presentation. Of course, the risk in this approach is that the speaker must be sure that he has held the attention of his audience throughout the entire presentation or his ending may fall on deaf ears.

Another way to present your key points is to begin with information that is already familiar to your audience and progress to the unfamiliar. For example, if you are trying to persuade a work team to undertake new responsibilities, you might begin by talking about the things they already do. This gives you an opportunity to praise them for their current work. It may also enable you to present their new duties as an extension of their existing responsibilities, which raises their comfort level — especially if they already feel overworked — and makes them more receptive to your proposals.

Presentation Organizing Plan

Central Message: Why managers must have effective presentation skills.

Most Important Point: Managers provide leadership in an organization. Communication skills enable them to chart a direction for other employees.

Second Key Point: Managers present new ideas, products and services to customers. These presentations must achieve maximum impact.

Third Key Point: Business meetings consume a large part of each day, and managers should know how to run them efficiently.

Fourth Key Point: Managers who make appearances before the media should represent their organizations effectively.

Practice Exercise
Practice the key point pattern with the following examples.

1. A talk explaining why flatter organizations are more successful in the marketplace.

_____
_____
_____
_____
_____
_____

2. A presentation about the benefits of a regular exercise program.

_____

_____

_____

_____

_____

3. A description of the new vision which you have developed for your department.

_____

_____

_____

_____

_____

COMBINATION OF PATTERNS:

The patterns just discussed can be extremely useful in organizing material to present to your audience. However, it is important to keep in mind that speakers frequently use more than one pattern in developing a presentation. For example, a vice president might begin by reviewing the step by step approach that was used for implementing a reorganization plan, then explain how the plan was carried out at each of the company's plant locations. Or a speaker might present the five key attributes of successful business writing, then present a step by step approach for acquiring these attributes, and finally explain why effective writing is so important at every level of an organization. Be careful to segue from one pattern to another, otherwise the flow of ideas can become confusing.

When you make a presentation, try to look for a pattern that fits your information most comfortably. You are likely to find that you can easily use several patterns in the same talk. This adds variety, which is an essential tool in keeping your audience involved. The patterns also provide a handy road map with familiar road signs that enable your listeners to follow the material that you are presenting to them. Finally, an organizing pattern can reduce the task of remembering what to say next. Simply follow the pattern. This will give you greater self-confidence as you stand up and speak in front of an audience.

 PATTERNS AND OUTLINES

Organizing patterns provide the basic outlines for a talk. An outline should remain informal. Do not get caught up in the formal process of Roman numerals and Arabic letters. Keep the outline simple — with main ideas that carry out the central message and give it meaning to the audience. Provide supporting information. Repetition of your central message and other key points can make it easier for your listeners to follow the information. Martin Luther King's "I Have a Dream" speech, for example, was made memorable by the use of this technique. In this case, King repeated his theme over and over to drive home the main point he wanted his listeners to remember.

 OUTLINE FOR YOUR PRESENTATION

1. Central Message 2. Meaning of the Message
3. Main Ideas 4. Supporting Information

_____

_____

_____

_____

_____

_____

_____

_____

_____

_____
_____
_____
_____
_____
_____
_____
_____
_____
_____
_____
_____
_____
_____
_____
_____
_____
_____
_____
_____
_____
_____
_____
_____
_____

Conclusion

1. Organizing material for a presentation can be difficult unless you use a pattern.

2. Several time-tested organizing patterns include: Chronology, Location, Hierarchy, Proposal-Benefits, Key Points.

3. Organizing patterns provide the basic outlines for talks.

CHAPTER FIVE

FINDING AN OPENING

Highlights

- *Use an effective opening or listeners will tune out*
- *Relate the opening to the central message*
- *Keep the opening brief*

"I once gave a presentation to senior executives and started with a funny story," a manager confessed. "At least, I thought it was funny. They said afterward I was being too informal and familiar with them. So unless you are really sure it's going to go over well, I would stay away from opening a talk with a joke."

"For me, it is the toughest part of a presentation," said a manufacturing executive, "coming up with a good opening."

One of the most challenging tasks confronting any speaker is how to open a talk. Indeed, some people find it so hard that they put together the rest of their talk first, and then come back to try to develop an opening. It used to be that the traditional way to open a talk was to tell a joke. In fact, it became so common place to begin a presentation with a joke, that this type of opening started to lose its impact.

Unfortunately, very few people are really good story tellers. They lack the proper sense of timing and their jokes often fall flat. Some speakers are so anxious to say something funny that they tell a joke that has little or nothing to do with the rest of the presentation. This simply throws the audience off course and fails to provide an effective lead in to the central message. Humor can also be quite subjective — what you find funny may not appeal to your listeners or they may feel it is inappropriate to the situation.

An acquaintance of ours, an attorney, recalls the following story: "I wanted to open a talk to my colleagues by telling a self-deprecating joke that poked fun at our profession and its tendency to equivocate whenever a client asks for a definitive answer. The punch line was going to be the standard advice that lawyers often give a client when he asks what to do — 'on the one hand and then on the other hand.' I stood up and was about to begin my talk, when I looked out into the audience. There in the third row sat an attorney with only one arm. Needless to say, I immediately had to change my opening."

> *"The greatest fault of a penetrating wit*
> *is to go beyond the mark."*
>
> *— La Rochefoucauld, 17th Century French Writer*

Whenever you think about leading off a presentation with a joke, be cautious. It is important to know the audience and the situation to make sure that the joke will fit both of them. That is not to say that you should never use a humorous opening. Humor can be very effective, especially when it pokes gentle fun at yourself and creates a bond between you and your audience. One approach is to point out a failing that all of you share, such as forgetfulness, for example, or a common experience that has probably happened to everyone, like daydreaming in meetings. Humor can often enable you to establish instant rapport with your audience and immediately draw them into your presentation. But you must use it appropriately.

ELEMENTS OF AN
EFFECTIVE OPENING

For years, television programs have opened with something that is known as a "teaser." At the top of the show they present dramatic or funny moments from the program to grab the viewers' attention. Producers know that if the audience is not hooked rapidly, they may tune out and begin channel surfing until they find something that truly interests them. In the same way, a speaker must make a good first impression on his audience or they may rapidly loose interest and tune out the central message. Part of this process is accomplished through visual skills, which we will discuss more thoroughly in a later chapter. How a speaker is dressed, for example, whether he looks directly at the audience and smiles at them — these things help to put listeners at ease and create an environment that is conducive to delivering a presentation. Of course, verbal skills — what the speaker says — are essential, too. And no part of a talk is more critical than the opening, the time when you make your first impression on the audience. Here are several criteria for developing a successful opening:

1. ***The opening should be tied to your central message.*** As explained earlier, a joke or funny story that bears no relation to your message simply confuses the audience. Good speakers present their central message early in a talk, generally as part of the opening or right after it. Therefore, they tie the message and the opening closely together so the audience is not led off the track.

2. ***Make the opening meaningful.*** A previous chapter talked about how the message should be relevant to your listeners. After all, the presentation is supposed to make an impact on them. The best place to begin is at the beginning. The opening should contain a nugget of information or some kernel of truth that will be relevant to your audience as well as related to your central message.

3. ***Keep it brief.*** Sometimes the speaker will begin with a story that
seems to go on forever. When at last he finishes, he may have
already lost his audience. Be sure you can make your point
quickly, in about a minute, then you can deliver your central message. Or it may be just as effective to deliver your central message first, then follow it up with an illustrative example.

4. ***Avoid cliches.*** Too often a speaker will begin with words such as
"Although I am unqualified to speak on this subject..." or "Unac-
customed as I am to speak in public..." or "I did not really have
much time to prepare today, but...." Cliches like these may make
you feel better, but your listeners really have no interest in them.
Indeed, they only serve to undermine your credibility as a speaker,
and, therefore, the significance of what you're trying to say. Make
the opening as memorable as possible, and you will be remembered by your listeners long after the presentation is completed.

5. ***Lead with power.*** Feature stories in a newspaper or magazine
usually begin with some anecdote that is related to the writer's
main point. For example, a story on flattening corporate hierarchies might open with an example of a self-directed work team at
a Fortune 500 company that cut cycle time in half and helped
boost profits 10 percent. This may be the most striking example
in the entire piece, which is why the writer put it up front. While
the anecdote relates to the central message, it may not relate directly to the first idea that the writer intends to present about that
message. Be prepared to present information out of order, if necessary, to make your talk as powerful as possible. It is essential
to hook the attention of your listeners as quickly as you can. This
usually means looking through all the anecdotes, examples, etc.
that you have collected for your talk and selecting the one that
will be most potent as a way of opening your presentation.

6. ***Take the time to prepare an effective opening.*** This is the place
where you hook the audience. If you begin with a flat opening, it
is much harder to hold the interest of your listeners as you present

the body of your talk. They may already be feeling let down, losing focus, and starting to think about something else. It may take some effort to find a powerful opening. Perhaps it already exists in the research you have done. If not, you may have to do some additional looking to discover a way to open the presentation. Sometimes, it helps to talk over your ideas with associates or family members. They may suggest an approach or tell you a story that will hit the mark.

Recently a participant in one of the Value Added Communications® seminars admitted: "I don't spend enough time thinking about what I am going to say or how I am going to say it." Give yourself enough time to create an opening that will capture the attention of your audience and make them want to know what you are going to tell them next.

TYPES OF OPENINGS

There are several effective ways to open a presentation. Your opening can include an anecdote or example that relates to your central message; you can begin with a relevant quotation or statistic; you can also start by asking your audience a question that is connected to the central message; or you can simply open by stating the message itself and following it up with a concrete example, statistic or anecdote.

Anecdotes & Examples

Recently, I read about the CEO of a major organization that had been experiencing financial problems. He was scheduled to leave for a short ski vacation to recharge his batteries and spend some time with his family. But on his first run down the mountain, he fell and dislocated his shoulder. The entire vacation seemed ruined. As it turned out, however, this unpleasant experience proved to be extremely fortuitous. A few days in the ski lodge gave the CEO time to gain a new perspective on the problems facing his company. He came back with a briefcase full of ideas that revitalized the organization and eventually helped it regain market share.

And that brings me to what I want to talk about today: How we can turn an unpleasant experience, such as the loss of a major account, into something that will provide the catalyst for turning around our entire department.

A good anecdote or example can immediately draw listeners into your presentation and capture their attention. Notice several things about this one. It is short and to the point. The story is related to the central message and the speaker ties both of them together. The example also provides the audience with a model to emulate, one that is designed to motivate them to take action. The speaker is saying: "If this CEO and his company can do it, then we can do it, too."

Here's a different type of anecdote:

Recently I have had conversations with several employees who have been talking to me about 'burn out.' One of them admitted to being so exhausted he could barely come in to work any longer. Another said that three downsizings had left her with so many responsibilities, she could not handle all of them. Today I want to discuss some ways of dealing with these problems.

Sometimes an historical anecdote or example can be used to open a presentation.

Almost a century ago, Henry Ford gave Americans an automobile of unrivaled quality that captured the marketplace. Once out in front with his Model T, however, Ford made the mistake of thinking he could stay there by simply manufacturing every car to look the same. But Americans' tastes were changing and they wanted cars that were stylish and colorful. For a time, Ford was caught flatfooted.

Change is nothing new, it has always been a constant in business. Over the years, many companies have learned that fact the hard way. Unless we know how to satisfy the changing tastes of our customers, we risk falling behind our competition.

> **Quotations**

Another useful tool for opening a presentation is a quotation. Sometimes a humorous quotation can break the ice so you can begin a discussion about a very serious subject.

To paraphrase writer Gelett Burgess, "If you have not discarded a major opinion or acquired a new one lately, check your pulse. You may be dead." Well, everyone in this audience looks very much alive to me. But, in checking the pulse of our operation, I do not think it is beating quite as fast as it might be. Indeed, many of you here in R&D have told me the same thing. What we need is to figure out a way to develop new ideas faster so they can reach the market-place sooner.

In this example, a little humor enables the speaker to open a meeting about how to revamp procedures in his department. You will notice that the quotation is also tied tightly to the central message of the presentation.

If you want to use this type of opening in your talk, be sure to make a habit of collecting relevant and interesting quotes in a file. It makes the process of finding an appropriate quotation much easier. I have personally found this to be much more effective than a book of familiar quotations which may have little or no material that relates to the topic which you are discussing.

Sometimes a quotation is very effective when it comes from a recognized authority in the field. In a speech on flattening organizational hierarchy, for example, a speaker might begin this way:

As General Electric's fabled CEO Jack Welch once put it: "We have been pulling the dandelions of bureaucracy for a decade, but they don't come up easily and they'll be back next week if you don't keep after them."

Startling Statistic

This is another successful way of opening a presentation. A statistic can not only focus your audience on what you are saying, it also lends credibility to your comments. Statistics can come form internal company surveys, newspaper and magazine articles, television and radio shows, as well as from sources such as the Internet. Here is an example:

Surveys show that the modern manager spends up to 40% of each day listening. Whether it is in staff meetings, telephone conversations with colleagues, face-to-face dialogues with subordinates, or sales calls on new customers, listening is always a key element of the communication process. Yet, how many of us are really effective listeners? According to one study, we listen with only 25% efficiency, and this accounts for the majority of misunderstandings that occur within our organizations.

That is why I want to spend some time in this workshop talking to you about how to improve your listening skills.

In this opening, the statistics underscore the importance of developing better listening skills and segue easily into the speaker's central message.

Asking A Question

This is an especially useful way of beginning a talk because it involves your audience almost immediately. But the question should meet several criteria:

1. It should lead directly into your central message. Otherwise you might open up a discussion with your audience that will take them away from the purpose of your presentation. For example, you might begin a seminar on oral communications by asking: *Why do you think it would be beneficial for you to become better speakers?* This is directly related to the purpose of your presentation.

2. The question should be non-controversial. Remember the question is designed to begin a dialogue with your audience, not to spark a debate. Keep the question simple and make sure you have a pretty good idea in advance how the audience will respond to it. If speaking about a new exercise program, for example, you might start this way: *How would you react if the company gave all of us an opportunity to become more physically fit and even gave us the time off we needed to use a new fitness program?*

3. Try to keep the responses short. A question can lead to a meaningful interaction with your audience, which is an essential part of any presentation. Nevertheless, be sure that your listeners keep their answers brief. Otherwise, the opening may continue for too long and distract the audience from the rest of your talk.

Some speakers like to use a rhetorical question as a device to persuade an audience of their point of view. In the 1980 presidential debates, for example, Ronald Reagan asked the now famous question: "Are you better off today than you were four years ago?" This helped him win the election.

You might open a talk this way: "Let me ask you a question: Are we doing everything possible to assure on-time deliveries to our customers?" You already know that the answer to this question is "no." What's more, you know that your audience realizes the same thing. However, you must be careful not to put the blame for an inadequate record of on-time deliveries on the shoulders of your listeners. This is the best way to lose them, almost before you begin.

Instead, you say that you and your listeners must share responsibility for the problem as well as its solution: "I'm sure that I could do a lot more to help our customers receive their orders on time. I'm sure all of us can. Now let's figure out how to do it together." You might then suggest ways that you and your listeners can deal with the problem. Thus, the rhetorical question helps you build a bridge to your audience so they can meet on common ground. This is an essential element in persuading them to take action.

**The Central
Message**

This is a straight forward, no-nonsense way of opening a presentation and telling listeners your purpose immediately. When used correctly, it ensures that your listeners clearly understand the purpose of your presentation. I feel it is the strongest, most direct and compelling means of opening your talk. Then, you should probably follow up with an anecdote, a statistic or a quote. This provides a concrete "for instance" that brings your central message to life by making it more specific. Here is an example:

If we want to be an innovative company in the 21st century, then we need a world class training program for our employees so they can acquire 21st century skills. Look at Acme Widget, for instance, where employees attend more hours of training than any other company in our region. Acme is a past winner of several prestigious quality awards as well as an acknowledged leader in its industry. Now, let us examine the steps we might follow to develop a training program like Acme's.

This talk opens with the central message, immediately followed by an example which serves as a benchmark for evaluating the company's training program. The example, the central message, and the transition sentence into the rest of the speech are tightly tied together.

There are several different ways to open presentations: anecdote, quotation, statistic, central message. You must decide which one will be most appropriate for your subject as well as most appealing to your audience.

Practice Exercises

Practice your speech openings with the following examples:

1. A central message for a talk explaining how an employee can improve his/her career in the organization.

_____

_____

_____

_____

2. A quotation to open a talk on how a crisis can lead to meaningful change.

_____

_____

_____

_____

3. A question to the audience to open a presentation on how employees might improve their problem solving skills.

_____

_____

_____

_____

4. A statistic that opens a speech on the need to make meetings shorter.

_____

_____

_____

_____

5. An anecdote introducing a presentation on the company's new health benefits program.

_____

_____

_____

_____

OPENING FOR YOUR PRESENTATION
Write an opening for the presentation which you
outlined in the previous chapter.

_____
_____
_____
_____
_____
_____
_____
_____
_____
_____
_____
_____
_____
_____
_____
_____
_____
_____
_____
_____
_____
_____
_____
_____
_____
_____
_____
_____
_____

Conclusion

1. Be cautious about opening a talk with a joke because it can fall flat.

2. Be sure to emphasize the central message in your opening.

3. Keep the opening brief and avoid cliches.

4. Be prepared to present information out of order, if necessary, to hook the audience with a powerful opening.

5. Several effective types of openings include: anecdotes, examples, quotations, startling statistics and asking a question.

CHAPTER SIX

STRATEGY FOR SUCCESS

Highlights

- *Use the 3 Ts to structure presentations*
- *Organizing patterns help you develop the body of a talk*
- *The conclusion enables you to reiterate your central message*

We talked to a group of managers and asked them if they could sum up in a few words what they're trying to accomplish when they give a presentation.

"I want to give my audience food for thought," one said, "without shoving it down their throats."

"I use a kind of marketing approach," another explained. "I try to figure out what it is I'm selling and why my audience would want to buy it. We all have to sell ideas."

"My approach is simple," said a third. "I want to make sure every-one understands the information I have to deliver. I tell them what I want to tell them. Tell them. Then tell them again. So my end is the beginning."

Successful speakers recognize that the amount of time they are given in which to influence an audience is limited, so they must make the most of it. This means the opening of their speech must engage the listeners as quickly as possible. Sometimes an interesting story will do the trick or perhaps a rhetorical question or even a joke, if it is appropriate to the situation. Once all eyes are on the speaker, then he must figure out a way to sustain his audience's interest. This chapter talks about developing the body and conclusion of a presentation, then organizing it into brief notes to be used in your delivery.

 ## STRUCTURING THE BODY
OF A TALK

The body is the meat of a presentation where the speaker should present rich "food for thought" or try to "sell ideas" to his listeners. Here, it is not only essential to keep your audience involved but also to make sure you keep them on track with the flow of your ideas and the logic of your arguments. How? With some very simple structural devices which will make their job of following you and what you are saying as easy as possible. Some speakers, like the one quoted above, use a very common device, often dubbed the 3Ts. In the opening, they tell the audience what they're going to tell them by presenting the central message. Then, in the body of the talk, the speaker tells them again by providing the details — ideas, anecdotes, statistics, etc — that flesh out the central message. Finally, in the conclusion, the speaker tells the audience what he told them, summarizing the central message and main ideas so his listeners won't forget them.

One of the finest presentations we ever heard followed exactly this approach. The speaker began by telling his listeners he was going to show them how to sell investment products to several different types of customers. Then he described each customer and how to design a sales pitch that would persuade them to buy his products. At the end, he briefly summarized these successful strategies. This overarching pattern will work with any kind of information. It gives you a number of opportunities to state and restate your central message throughout the presentation, which is its great advantage.

The 3Ts are like a blueprint. While it may be essential to building a house, a blueprint will only take you so far. You also need the bricks and mortar, the walls and roofing that will hold the building together. Chapter Four described various types of structures for organizing a presentation. These structures are especially useful in tying up the various pieces that form the body of your presentation into a logical whole that should be easy for your audience to understand.

Here is an example of the chronological structure. Suppose you were speaking about the five steps in developing an effective proposal. You open with an anecdote about a colleague who received funding for a new project because the submitted proposal was very persuasive and well-written. Then you present your central message: "Your proposals will stand a much better chance of being approved if you follow these five steps."

At this point, you segue into the body of your presentation: "Step one is to define the purpose of your proposal. You'd be surprised how many people seem unclear about the purpose and cannot sum it up in a few words." You might follow this statement with a statistic on the number of proposals that are turned down in your organization each year, how much competition there is to have proposals accepted, and why a clearly defined purpose is such an important element in a well-written proposal. Then you might offer some examples of what you mean.

The next part of the body might begin this way: "Step two is to gather all the data you need to support your purpose. This may sound like a formidable task, but let me show you some ways to make it simpler." The rest of this section might delineate the specific ways you have in mind.

Notice that the body of this presentation is held together by very simple connecting devices which arise from your organizing struc-

ture: Step 1, Step 2, etc. These words provide transitions between
various sections of the body and make your talk much easier to follow for everyone in the audience.

> **Organizing
> Your Talk
> Into Notes**

A tight organizational structure, like the one just
described, can easily be transferred into notes to
be used in preparing and rehearsing your presentation. For example, each step in developing a proposal can include key words for the anecdotes, statistics, etc., which provide your supporting information. At the end
of each section, you also have an opportunity to reiterate your central message by stating how critical this particular step is to a well-
executed proposal. You would be amazed how much your listeners
will appreciate a presentation that is so carefully organized for them
and how much simpler it will be for you to deliver.

Here is another example. Suppose you are planning to speak about
the efforts of your organization to revitalize the city in which its
headquarters are located. You decide to open with an anecdote in-
volving several employees who are involved in a mentoring program at a local elementary school, citing the satisfaction they have
derived from helping children in math and science. Then you present
your central message and segue into the rest of your talk: "The
mentoring program is only one example of the enormous commitment that we are making to improve this city. Our commitment involves several different initiatives, including volunteer activities,
partnering with ongoing community development programs here in
the city, and efforts to attract outside financial resources for urban
renewal."

The body of the presentation might now be organized into the key
points pattern discussed in chapter four. Here is a sample.

*First, I would like to talk about the volunteer programs that have
received such strong support from our employees. Did you know
that fully 65% of the people who work here are now engaged in some
type of volunteering in the city? That is a terrific record. Several*

employees serve in the mentoring program at Howe Elementary School, which I mentioned in the opening of my talk. This year, three of our engineers — Bill Watson, Janice Harrison, and Anna Gonzales — helped the school stage its annual science fair. There were forty-eight different exhibits. Bill, Janice and Anna served as judges, awarding gift certificates from a local toy store to the winners. We also have a very active Literacy Volunteers Program, which was started several years ago by Jane Douglas and currently includes 75 employees who devote two hours each week to tutoring adults. In addition, our company sponsors a Little League team, the Chiefs, and one of the coaches is our own vice president for marketing, Wayne Macaluso. I am proud to say that this team just completed its season and finished second in the standings. But Wayne assures me that next year he expects them to win the division...

Your notes for this section of the talk might look this way:

Opening
Anecdote: Anne Carlson and James Jackson mentoring children at Howe Elementary School.
Central Message: Our commitment to improve the city which involves 3 initiatives—volunteer activities, partnering, efforts to attract outside financial resources.

I. Volunteer Activities
Statistic: 65% of employees involved in volunteering
Howe: Repeat mentoring program.
Science Fair—Bill Watson, Janice Harrison, Anna Gonzales
Judge contest and award prizes
Literacy volunteers—Jane Douglas; 75 employees; 2 hours per week
Little League team—Wayne Macaluso. Finished 2nd in standings
Repeat central message

In the second part of the body of your presentation, you would discuss the company's efforts to partner with community development
groups.

*This brings me to the second initiative we have undertaken:
partnering with local groups to support community renewal. In the
north end of the city, for example, we have been working with the
Hilltop Partnership to create an area of low and middle income housing as well as a magnate school for the arts. So far a total of 60
units have been completely rehabilitated.*

*As part of a special "Paint the Town" program, a group of volun-
teers from the company, led by our maintenance supervisor, Jack
LaRoche, painted a number of these houses themselves. We are currently trying to arrange loans to build the magnate school and I'll
have more to say about that in a few moments.*

*Down in the south end, our manufacturing plant established an ap-
prenticeship program three years ago which is providing training
for high school students in the afternoons following their classes.*

*Harry Lauther, one of the supervisors at the plant, and Hector
Rodriguez, an apprentice, will give you a short presentation about
the program after I have finished. We've also worked hard to create
more jobs by contracting with local suppliers, whenever possible.*

*Right around the corner from headquarters, we are involved in an-
other housing project....*

This section of the talk is organized by the location pattern discussed
earlier. Your notes might look this way:

II. Partnering

North End— Hilltop Partnership; 60 low and middle income housing units; magnate school for the arts "Paint the Town:" Jack LaRoche, painting houses

South End— Apprenticeship program for high school students;Harry Lauther and Hector Rodriguez to make presentation; efforts to use local suppliers

Near Headquarters—Housing project

A similar approach might be used if you were preparing notes for a presentation in which the material was organized according to one of the other structural patterns, **hierarchical**, for example, or **proposal/benefits**. These patterns provide a tight framework for the body of your presentation. Another way to tie the body together is by repetition, repeating the central message, for instance, at the end of each section. You can also introduce the sections in the opening of your talk, then repeating each section as you get to it in the body of your presentation. Finally, you can tie the body together by using various transitional words and phrases such as:

"In the north end, in the south end, etc..."

"Now that I have finished with that section, let me go on to the next one..."

"First, second, third, etc...." *"Step 1, Step 2, Step 3, etc..."*

"In addition to the benefits I have just discussed, my proposal has another one...."

"This completes our discussion of quality improvements in the manu-facturing area, let's turn now to customer service...."

While these devices may seem a bit artificial, they provide essential road signs that help your listeners follow the course of your presentation. Remember, you are the one who organized the speech and you know far more about the flow of the information than your audience does. Any assistance you can provide will only increase the chances that your message will be heard and understood.

Here is a short excerpt from a talk, followed by the notes on which it was based.

    PRESENTATION EXCERPT

Anecdote   It's 3 P.M. You're sitting in a plush meeting room while the speaker slowly unveils his marketing program for the company during the coming year. It has been a long day, and gradually your mind begins to wander from the speaker's presentation to other topics, such as last night's tennis game, or perhaps the vacation you are planning later in the summer. Suddenly, you realize that the people sitting next to you are smiling and nodding their heads knowingly in agreement. The speaker has just made the most important point of his presentation and you were not listening.

Central Message/ Meaning   This type of experience has probably happened to everyone of us. How many meetings do you attend every day? How many times have you missed a key point in a meeting? One way to avoid this problem is to develop your listening skills and use them successfully. It will help all of you become better managers. Today I want to suggest several ways to improve these skills.

Body:
Section I

First, try to beat the boredom trap. Many people are forced to attend dry, detailed presentations on topics that hold very little interest for them. And they often wonder how they can keep themselves from being bored and tuning out the speaker. The answer is simple: Find something in the speech that can help you. Listen carefully to what the speaker has to say. Then keep asking yourself how it can benefit you.

Perhaps you will learn something that improves the way you do your job, or run your department or plan for retirement. You'll be surprised how many valuable nuggets of information you can uncover if you just listen.

Body:
Section II

Another approach to improving your listening skills is this: Don't jump to conclusions. You know, the average speaker talks at about 160 words per minute, but we can absorb information at more than three times that rate. So it's easy to stop paying attention.

Suppose you're listening to a colleague describe a new reorganization plan for your department. You disagree with the plan, but instead of listening to all the arguments supporting it, you immediately jump ahead and begin developing your own rebuttal.

Resist the temptation to jump to conclusions. Make
sure you listen to the entire presentation and clearly
understand all the main points. Who knows, you
may even find yourself agreeing with some of
them. But even if you don't, you are in a much
better position to present an effective rebuttal. It
is one more advantage to sharpening your listening skills.

Body:
Section III

Almost 2000 years ago, the philosopher Epictetus
was among the first to put listening in its proper
perspective. He said: "Nature has given to man
one tongue, but two ears, that we may hear from
others twice as much as we speak." But in order
to listen effectively, we must concentrate on the
speaker. This is the third approach to improving
your listening skills.

Studies show that the major cause of poor listening is not noise, or poor acoustics, but a failure of
concentration. One way to improve your concentration is to take notes while you are attending a
meeting or listening to a speech. Do not try to write
down all the details, most of them are probably
unimportant. Listen only for the main ideas and
jot them down. This will help your concentration....

The notes might look this way:

Opening

Anecdote: Person begins daydreaming in meeting. Thinks about tennis game, vacation. Suddenly sees everyone smiling and nodding and realizes he has missed most important point.

Central Message: How many times have we missed a key point because of all the meetings we attend? Importance of improving listening skills, suggest several ways to improve them.

Meaning: Better listening skills mean better managers.

I. Beat the Boredom Trap

Find something in the speech that can help you.
Listen carefully and find the benefits: doing your job better, running your department better, planning for retirement.

II. Do Not Jump to Conclusions

Statistic: Speaker talks at 160 wpm; we listen at 3 times that rate. It is easy to stop paying attention

Example: Colleague proposes reorganization plan; you disagree, but instead of listening, you start planning a rebuttal. Listen to entire presentation, understand main points (you may agree with some of them). If not, you are still better prepared to rebut.

Repeat Central Message

III. Concentrate on the Speaker

Quote: Epictetus- "Nature has given to man one tongue, but two ears that we may hear from others twice as much as we speak."

Lesson: To listen effectively, you must concentrate.

How to concentrate: Take notes — main ideas only, not all the details.

Practice Exercise

Practice organizing the opening and the body of a talk into brief notes with one of the following examples:

1. The advantages of living in your community.
2. How to be an effective volunteer.
3. The process of finding a new job.

Opening

_____

_____

_____

_____

_____

_____

Section I

_____

_____

_____

_____

_____

_____

Section II

_____

_____

_____

_____

_____

_____

BODY FOR YOUR PRESENTATION

Using the presentation which you have been developing in previous chapters, organize the opening and the body into short notes.

Opening

_____
_____
_____
_____
_____
_____

Section I

_____
_____
_____
_____
_____

Section II

_____
_____
_____
_____
_____

Section III

_____
_____
_____
_____
_____

CREATING CONCLUSIONS

The conclusion of a talk is your final opportunity to make a lasting impression on an audience. Do not let it slip away. Some speakers reach the end of their presentations and sound as if they have run out of gas. They complete the body of their talk and suddenly say to the audience: "Well, I guess that's all I have to say on this subject," or "That brings me to the end of my talk. Thank you very much." Then, they abruptly walk away from the podium. This leaves the audience hanging in mid air. They feel let down. The speech seems unfinished, as if it is lacking something important...something that belongs at the end to give it a final impact.

What belongs at the end? The conclusion is a time to reiterate your central message and the meaning of the message — "to tell them what you told them." This insures that the audience receives the message that you are trying to deliver.

Real listening is perhaps the most important, yet most misunderstood of all the communication skills. It is not a haphazard activity that requires only our partial attention. It demands our total involvement with the speaker. This is not an easy task, because we're not trained to be good listeners. Yet everyone can learn the skills which I have just outlined in this talk. And the rewards both personally and professionally can be enormous.

In addition to the central message, you might also include a quotation, anecdote or statistic to give the conclusion more power and make it even more meaningful for your listeners.

As one manager told me: "Listening helps me build rapport with other people, especially my subordinates. And that is the key to effective leadership."

Some speakers choose to end a presentation with a question. This can be extremely powerful if you want to persuade your audience to take action.

Can we all become better listeners? Yes, I think we can.

or

How many of you want to be better listeners? (audience raises their hands) Then, let's start today.

CONCLUSION FOR YOUR PRESENTATION
Write the notes for the conclusion to the presentation
which you have been developing.

_____

_____

_____

_____

_____

_____

_____

_____

_____

_____

_____

_____

_____

_____

_____

_____

_____

_____

_____

_____

_____

_____

_____

_____

Conclusion

1. Some speakers structure a presentation by using the 3Ts: Tell the audience what you want to tell them; tell them; then tell them again at the end of the talk.

2. The body of a presentation can be held together by using various structures (chronology, location, key points, etc.) as well as simple connecting devices, such as, Step 1, Step 2, etc.

3. An organizational structure can easily be transferred into notes to be used in preparing and rehearsing your presentation.

4. The conclusion of a presentation is your last chance to make a lasting impression on the audience.

5. In the conclusion, reiterate your central message and the meaning of the message.

CHAPTER SEVEN

VISUALIZE YOUR WAY TO VICTORY

Highlights

- *You are your most important visual aid*
- *Keep visuals simple and brief*
- *Use only a minimum of visuals*

A mid-level manager had spent several weeks preparing a presentation for the head of his department. As he walked toward the front of the conference room, tightly grasping a huge stack of overheads, he knew that all eyes were upon him. He could not afford to fail as far too much was riding on the next twenty minutes. But as he neared the podium, the manager suddenly felt himself trip and stumble. Using all the effort available to him, he somehow managed to recover his footing and avoid a humiliating fall. However, he had lost control of the overheads, which flew into the air, scattering on the floor in front of him. Without them, he could neither remember nor deliver his presentation. After a delay, he was able to reorganize the visuals and proceed with the presentation. Although he suffered little more than a bruised ego, it was enough to cause him extreme embarrassment in front of his boss, and did nothing to enhance his reputation in the department.

Today, presentations frequently include visual aids. These might consist of such things as overheads, slides, graphics shown directly from a computer, or videotapes. Unfortunately, some speakers, have come to rely completely on visual aids to make their presentations. They arrive with an armful of overheads, and the entire talk is comprised of projecting one after another, while they read them aloud to the audience. Frankly, they could just as easily have stayed home and sent hard copies of their visual aids. This would have saved everyone a great deal of time and trouble, to say nothing of preventing the speaker from suffering the embarrassment of having a presentation canceled because the visual aids fell all over the floor or because the equipment to show them malfunctioned.

As a speaker, you are your most important visual aid. The audience comes to hear *you*, see *you*, and interact with *you*. If you want to hold their attention, the best way to do it is with the power of your words, and the strength of your delivery. Visual aids are just that, aids. While they can play an important role in presenting information, it should only be in a supportive role for you, the speaker. Too often, visual aids seem to take center stage, and the speaker is relegated to the background. Instead, you should always remain front and center.

This is not to say that visuals cannot enhance your presentation. Studies show that they add interest to a talk, improve recall among your listeners, and even reduce the amount of time you have to spend presenting information. However, this is true only if the visual aids are used effectively! Here are a few things to remember the next time you decide to include visuals in your presentation.

Less is more. So keep the number of visual aids to a minimum. One picture may be worth a thousand words, but too many can be overwhelming and their impact will be lost on your audience. Visual aids should not substitute for your presentation. They should simply reinforce key ideas and basic concepts. Therefore, prepare only the number of visuals you need to accomplish this goal.

Convey only one central idea for each visual aid. A visual with too much information will only confuse your audience. In an experiment conducted in one of our classes, we asked each of the presenters whether they needed all the information contained on their visual aids. Each of them said "yes." However, the perception of the audience was quite different. All of them agreed that the visual aids contained far too much material to be effective.

Include only the necessary information. Each visual aid should have a title, which acts as a headline, telegraphing the main idea. Make the headline short and punchy. If the rest of the visual contains only words, keep them to a minimum — five or six lines at the most — and all of them should support the main idea. If you're presenting a graph or chart, one per visual is usually about all that your audience will be able to absorb. Keep the chart simple. (We will discuss some of the guidelines for creating simple, clear graphics later in this chapter.)

Make sure the information is readable. Too often a speaker will try to present a page from a book on an overhead. This is almost impossible for the audience to read clearly. A good rule of thumb is to put the overhead on the floor and stand over it. If you can read the print, then it is large enough for the audience to see. With slides, hold them at arm's length from you. If you cannot read the type, then it is too small.

Plan your visual aids. Figure out how the visuals can best support the central message and the meaning of your message. Then, leave yourself enough time to prepare the visual aids carefully. One manager said that at least half his time in getting ready for a presentation is devoted to developing visual aids. While this may be a bit excessive, it emphasizes the importance of proper preparation. Some speakers keep a visual aid file. This reduces the need to produce all new visual materials every time they make a presentation. You can organize the file by subject or by the date when the visuals were shown.

Vary the types of visual aids. While word visuals are the most popular, if you use nothing else, they can become extremely monotonous. Vary your visual aids by including charts and graphs. Computer software now enables you to create these visuals very easily. Software packages include a variety of templates for such things as pie charts, bar graphs, line graphs, and scatter diagrams. You can simply type in your information, and the software organizes it into a graph. Then you can select appropriate sizes and styles of type as well as colorful backgrounds for your visuals.

TYPES OF VISUALS

WORDS
These are the visual aids that you are most likely to see during a presentation. The best visuals are generally the simplest. They contain a short headline that communicates the main idea and a few lines of bullet points.

LISTENING SKILLS
- Focus on the message
- Concentrate
- Don't jump to conclusions
- Ask questions

The headline might be presented in all capital letters or in upper and lower case. No matter which you choose, it is important to remain consistent throughout the remainder of your visuals. After your audience sees the first visual aid, they expect the rest of them to maintain the same consistency of style. Anything else will be distracting and take their attention away from the information that you are trying to communicate. Generally the body text of a visual is presented in upper and lower case, because this is the format that audiences have become accustomed to seeing when they read information in a printed format.

If you're preparing a word visual on your computer, it is important to make the type large enough for your audience to read. Ten point type is much too small. On an overhead, for example, graphics experts recommend 14 point type which is the size frequently used for the text in books and other printed materials. These experts also suggest that you keep the style of type as simple as possible. You don't want to have your listeners thinking about the fancy type design you chose instead of concentrating on your presentation.

A sans-serif, such as Helvetica or Optima, is excellent for projected visuals because it is bold and easy to read. Sans-serif means without the little flairs and finishing strokes that come at the end of letters. By contrast, serif type faces are widely used in newspapers and books, because they are best for presenting a body of text. Here again, consistency is important. Select a type style and stay with it throughout the presentation.

If you want to emphasize specific words on your visual, the use of boldface or a color can create a powerful effect. But we recommend that you utilize these techniques sparingly. If overused, they quickly lose their impact. Computer software enables you to select a wide variety of colors for the type and backgrounds of your visuals, and in the right combinations they can carry enormous eye appeal.

Visual aids generally seem to work best when a dark background is combined with lighter type. Examples might be yellow or white type on a navy or dark green background. You can also select another color for bullets used to set off each point that appears on the visual.

Word slides are most effective when lines are kept short. Each one should use consistent phrasing — eg. all commands, or all adjectives and nouns, etc.

Review the following example:

ELEMENTS OF SUCCESSFUL MEETINGS

- Do you allow plenty of time to prepare for a meeting or do you leave it to the last minute?
- Clear, concise agendas without any confusion about the topics to be discussed among the participants.
- Emphasize participation and your meetings will be far more effective because the audience will be involved.

Each of these bullets is much too long and uses a different type of phrasing, which is confusing for the audience. The first line is a question; the second consists of a couple of adjectives modifying the noun "agendas," which is followed by several phrases; and the last bullet point is presented as a command. The visual might be much more effective if it were presented this way.

ELEMENTS OF SUCCESSFUL MEETINGS

- Effective preparation
- Clear, concise agendas
- Employee participation

Now each line is short and the phrasing is consistent, with an adjective and noun for every bullet point. The visual presents only the highlights, then the speaker can expand upon each of them during the presentation.

Practice Exercises

Practice creating brief bullet points with consistent phrasing by rewriting the following statements about meetings:

1. You should develop a theme to give the meeting a focus and concentrate everyone's energies.

2. A dialogue with your listeners to keep them involved and motivated so they will pay attention.

---

3. Do you conclude with an action plan to bring closure to the meeting?

---

4. Keep the meetings as short as possible, centered on a specific agenda, with clearly defined objectives.

---

5. Visual aids that present your main ideas concisely and with a maximum of impact.

---

6. Rehearsing — it can spell the difference between failure and success.

TABLES. Another way to present information is in the form of a simple table. For example:

CHANGES IN EMPLOYEE POPULATION		
	Layoffs	New Hires
Company A	10,000	1500
Company B	25,000	3000
Company C	5,000	500

In designing tables, type is generally presented flush left while numbers are displayed flush right. It's also a good idea to leave some space between the horizontal and vertical lines so they do not run together. Some speakers place rules between the horizontal lines to give them further definition. Adding a light color to the rules, and setting the data against a dark color background, can give the entire chart more impact. Computers also enable you to add an icon to a chart to make it more interesting. For example, it you are talking about employee layoffs, you can add a picture of an employee to the chart to give it greater visual appeal.

If the table includes numbers with decimal points, these should be aligned by the decimal to make them easier for your audience to read. Otherwise, they might still be trying to figure out your table while you are talking and miss the point.

PRODUCTION REPORT	
Plant	Units
Center City	15.6
East End	12.5
Long Hill	18.4
Great Park	9.3

BAR GRAPHS. Bar graphs are a simple, attractive way to present comparisons among several items. Horizontal bar graphs, for example, enable you to compare things at a specific point in time.

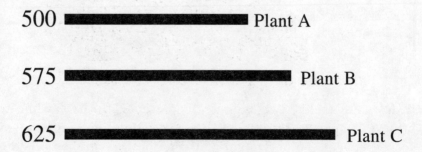

500 ▬▬▬▬▬▬▬▬ Plant A

575 ▬▬▬▬▬▬▬▬▬ Plant B

625 ▬▬▬▬▬▬▬▬▬▬ Plant C

Vertical bar graphs present comparisons between items at various points in time. The vertical axis usually indicates the quantities of each item being compared while the horizontal axis presents the different time intervals under consideration. Instead of a solid bar, some speakers like to use icons to represent the quantities that they are discussing. For example, if you were talking about the number of televisions produced in several plants, you might create each bar in a graph out of small TV sets. This would make the chart more interesting for your audience. One popular form of the vertical bar graph is the so-called stacked bar graph. This can be used to compare several items at several different points in time. If you were giving a presentation discussing sales figures in various territories throughout the year, you might use a stacked bar graph to depict some of the information.

SALES BY TERRITORY

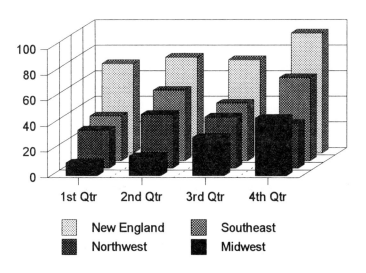

PIE CHARTS. These popular graphics are used for presenting parts of a whole. The whole should always total up to 100%. Each part can be portrayed in a different color, allowing it to stand out for the audience. Percentages can be placed inside each section or on the outside. One note of caution: Do not slice the pie too thin. Once I attended a presentation in which the speaker projected a pie chart with three sections in the top two-thirds; and sixteen sections in the bottom. I could not read them, and I'm sure everyone else in the audience experienced the same problem. (This problem can also occur with bar charts.)

Suppose you were presenting a recent survey about the impact of various plant closings in your area on family finances. The survey data, showing how many families had seen their incomes fall behind, stay the same, or move ahead, might look this way:

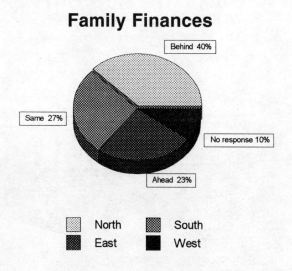

A variation of this type of chart is the exploded pie chart. Speakers may use this type of graphic when they want to draw the audience's attention to one particular part of a pie chart.

Family Finances

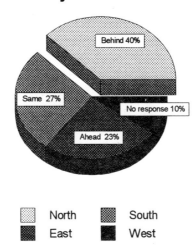

	North		South
	East		West

LINE GRAPHS. Line graphs are the direct descendants of the fever charts that began being used in hospitals many years ago to monitor the ups and downs in a patient's temperature. These graphs are excellent at showing changes in profits, production units, new hires, etc., over a period of time. The lines enable the viewer to see the flow, whether up, down or flat, and each point represents a particular point in time at which a measurement was taken. By using a computer to present the graphic during a presentation, the lines can be animated, making the flow even more apparent to the audience.

Profits per Division

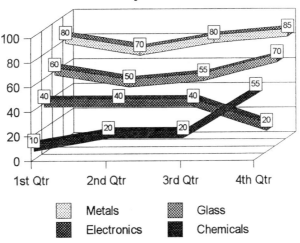

	Metals		Glass
	Electronics		Chemicals

THE MEDIA MIX

Visual aids can be presented in a variety of formats. Computers, for example, play a key role not only in creating visuals but in presenting them, as well. For small groups, say three or four people, visual aids can be displayed directly on a computer screen from your laptop. For larger groups, your computer can be hooked up to a liquid crystal display (LCD), which is clamped onto an overhead projector that displays the visuals on a large screen. Since some LCDs do not have an especially high resolution, it is essential that your graphics, particularly words and numbers, be just as bold and crisp as possible.

Computers enable you to present vivid and colorful visuals on the screen. You can also change the visual aids during your talk in response to additional input from your audience. However, do not let yourself become so enamored of the computer that it overshadows you as the speaker. Visual aids are only there to support what you have to say, not take the place of it. Too often, speakers who base a presentation entirely on computer graphics, discover to their horror that the equipment does not work properly or there is a glitch in the software. As a result, they are left high and dry.

Another medium for presenting visual aids is video. This can be an excellent format if you have to demonstrate a fluid process, such as how a piece of manufacturing equipment operates or how to repair the equipment when it breaks down. Video can be used with a small group of people looking at a television monitor or or it can be shown to a larger audience with a big screen projection system. One of the problems, however, is that the viewers may have a tendency to daydream while the videotape is being shown.

Video is a passive medium, as well as a very expensive one to produce. Therefore, it should be used judiciously as a visual aid. Short pieces, of only a few minutes, usually work best when they are presented to introduce new concepts or demonstrate a process. Then turn off the video and continue with the rest of your presentation, while you still have the attention of your audience.

For the past half-century, slides have been a widely used visual aid and they show no signs of declining in popularity. As a speaker support, slides present clear, crisp images to large audiences of fifty or more. The same computer software that generates these images can also produce a hard copy of the slides (to be used as handouts for your audience).

If the slides contain only the key points of your talk, as they should, the handouts will enable your listeners to walk away with a valuable written record that can be used to review the presentation highlights. For the handouts, you should also include more material than what appears on the slides. This will give your audience an even better version to study after your talk.

Whenever you present slides, do not let yourself stay glued to the projector. This not only forces you to speak over the noise of the fan, but it also prevents you from looking at the audience, since the projector is usually located somewhere in the middle or back of the conference room. Instead, use a remote control device that allows you to change slides while you are standing next to them. In this manner, you can point to a slide and discuss it while continuing to directly address the audience, thus you and the visual are now working together.

The most widely used format for presenting visual aids continues to be the overhead, also called a viewgraph or foil. The overheads can be created by hand, or more professionally, with computer software. It is a good idea to number them in case they get out of order. Overheads work best with a group of forty or fifty people. If you are using overheads as visual aids, here are a few tips to keep in mind:

1. *Begin by putting the foil on the glass and turning on the overhead projector.* As you walk back to the screen, look at the visual and think about what you want to say.

2. *Do not start describing the visual to the audience as you walk toward the screen.* It is not only discourteous to talk to your listeners with your back turned to them, it is also more difficult for them to hear what you're saying.

3. *Once you are looking at the audience, give them an overview of the entire visual before discussing any of its details.* This gives your listeners a chance to orient themselves, allowing them to understand the "forest" before you start to focus on the "trees." For example, if you are projecting a pie chart that shows a breakdown of company profits for the year, introduce the title of the visual aid and provide a brief overview of it before discussing the profits contributed by each division.

4. *As you talk, stay next to the screen.* This allows the audience to look at you and the visual aid simultaneously. If you move too far away from the visual, your audience's attention will be split between you and the overhead.

5. *It is also best to stand to the left of the visual aid.* People naturally read from left to right, so they can look from you to the visual and back again.

6. *Do not lean across the visual as you try to point to a detail on it.* This only puts you directly in front of the light and part of the visual aid will be projected on you. Instead, point to a specific detail or refer to it with words such as, "on the far right side, you can see_____", etc.

7. *Once you have finished discussing the visual aid, step forward to the projector and turn it off.* Your listeners should now give their full attention to you and not be distracted by a visual that has already been fully discussed.

8. ***Do not turn on the projector and present the next visual until you are ready to talk about it.*** Otherwise, your audience will be looking at a visual aid that is not supporting what you are saying.

Some of these same points are useful to remember no matter what type of visual aid you decide to include in your next presentation. Visuals are tools which can add variety and provide more zest to your talks. They reinforce main ideas, demonstrate procedures, present data in graphs and charts, making it more easily understandable. Each of these tools requires a skilled presenter who knows how to utilize them successfully so they can make a significant impact on an audience. This means that you must plan your visuals carefully, determining where to use them so they support your main ideas, deciding which type of visual to use (graphs, charts, slides, overheads, etc.) and preparing what you are going to say about each of them. These are essential steps in creating winning presentations.

VISUAL AID PLANNER
Develop the visual aids for the presentation that
you have been creating.

MAIN IDEA　　　　　　　**VISUAL**

1.

2.

3.

Conclusion ──────────────

1. As a speaker, you are your most important visual aid.

2. When you create visual aids, keep their number to a minimum; convey only one central idea on each visual; include only the necessary information. Make sure all the information is readable. If you use more than one visual, vary the types of visual aids.

3. In preparing word visuals, make sure the type is simple and readable and the lines are short.

4. In designing tables, type is generally presented flush left while numbers are displayed flush right.

5. Bar graphs are a simple, attractive way to present comparisons among several items.

6. Pie charts are popular graphics used for presenting parts of a whole.

7. Line graphs show changes over time.

8. Visual aids can be presented in a variety of formats, including slides, video, on computer screens or on overheads.

CHAPTER EIGHT

MASTERING THE
GIVE & TAKE

Highlights

- *Begin a dialogue with your audience*
- *Open-ended questions are excellent for audience involvement*
- *Q&A sessions also encourage listener participation*

One manager asks: *"How can I hold the attention of a group when I have to give a rather lengthy presentation?"*

"I can tell the audience loses interest part of the way through my talk," laments another manager. *"How can I keep them involved?"*

"Every time I give a speech," admits a third executive, *"it's a non-stop monologue, which frankly tires me out and probably bores the audience. How can I change that?"*

The answers to all of these questions can best be summed up in a single phrase: *"Audience participation."*

A century and half ago Margaret Fuller went on the public lecture circuit at a time when women were usually expected to stay at home and confine their speech-making to friends and relatives. She called

her lectures "conversations." The lectures were not only intended to
present her own viewpoints on topics such as philosophy and reli-
gion, but they were also designed to elicit responses from her audiences, who were encouraged to express their opinions freely and
discuss them with the speaker. In an era when most speakers were
content to stand on the podium and talk interminably while their
listeners were expected to pay strict attention, Margaret Fuller presented a somewhat unique approach to speech making, one that involved her audiences. She drew them into her presentations.

Today, how many of us think of a talk the way Margaret Fuller did,
as anything other than a monologue in which we do all of the talking
and the audience is there to simply sit back and listen or at most take
a few notes? But what a burden this puts on the speaker! You are
responsible for every idea, every word, every sentence. It's enough
to make anyone feel anxious and probably accounts for a large percentage of the stage fright that afflicts so many people. Unless the
speaker is extremely polished, these types of presentations are often
deadly because the audience remain passive observers. They feel no
stake in what is happening in front of them because they are not
participating in it. Have you ever tried to pay attention to someone
who never stops talking at you, who never gives you a chance to get
a word in edgewise? After a while, you simply tune out. It's often
the same with audiences who are forced to sit through a lecture.

> *"If for the sake of an audience, you do wish to hold a*
> *lecture, your ambition is no laudable one...."*
> *—Hippocrates*

Many of your listeners would probably welcome an opportunity to
break out of the usual mold of making talks. Instead of you, the
speaker, doing all the talking, the audience can add its own input
into what is being said. It would give them a chance to express their
viewpoints, ones that might enhance your talk. At the same time, it
would also take an enormous burden off you to present all the infor-

mation yourself. Nowhere is it written in stone that when you deliver a talk you must do all the work. Encourage your audience to participate!

 ## BEGIN A DIALOGUE

One of the best ways of promoting audience involvement is to begin a dialogue with your listeners. How? Just as you might start a conversation with someone you have met for the first time at a cocktail party, ask a question. The most effective types of questions are open-ended ones because they give other people the chance to talk a bit about what is on their minds. Close-ended questions, on the other hand, often close down a dialogue almost before it has begun.

For example, suppose you are talking about the benefits of increased workforce diversity in your organization. Let us say you ask the audience this question: "What percentage of women do you think are currently in our upper management ranks?" This is a close-ended question for which there is only a single, short response. It does not promote a discussion. On the contrary, unless your listeners actually knew the answer, they would be hesitant to offer any information at all, for fear it might be incorrect and they would expose their ignorance in front of their peers. By contrast, you might ask: "How do you think increased workforce diversity might benefit our department?" or "How do you think it would benefit our customers?" Either of these would easily solicit a wide range of opinions. There is no right or wrong answer to these questions. They are designed to encourage people to talk, express their viewpoints, and participate in your presentation. This increases their level of interest and enthusiasm in what you are saying, because they now feel a part of it.

Dialogue questions can be used at various points throughout your presentation to keep the audience involved. Instead of trying to think of them on the spur of the moment while your talk is underway, you should probably develop several questions in advance, as one of the steps in your preparation. Some speakers are reluctant to ask questions because they are afraid that no one in the audience might respond. If there is not an immediate response to one of your dialogue questions, don't panic. Sometimes your listeners need a few seconds to think about the question and decide what they want to say. If, after a brief pause, no one has still volunteered to make a reply, you might be tempted to ask a specific person. Unfortunately this often puts someone on the spot, which might prove embarrassing if he has no answer to the question. Instead, you might give your audience a hint. For example, suppose you were talking about the task of balancing work and family life. You then asked your listeners what the most challenging aspect of this task was. If no one immediately responded, you might say: "For me, it's dealing with the stress I feel when I need to stay late at work and knowing that my children need me at home." This type of "prompt" or "hint" will usually start the dialogue rolling and encourage your listeners to participate.

Try to involve as many listeners as possible, without letting the dialogue go on for too long. After the discussion has been underway for a few minutes, bring it to a successful conclusion so you can proceed with the rest of your presentation. You might say: "I wish we could continue with this a little longer, but I have to get back to my talk." At this point, you should briefly summarize what the listeners have said, relate it to your central message, and segue back into your presentation.

Here is a short excerpt from a presentation on volunteering that demonstrates the use of dialogue questions.

PRESENTATION EXCERPT

Anecdote   This fall I began my third season as a tour guide
                    at our community Nature Center, and I noticed that
                    something was different. There were far more
                    guides than ever before. In fact, someone told me

that for the first time the center didn't need to advertise for guides because people simply volunteered.

Anecdote

Recently, a headline in our local newspaper read: "Volunteerism is restoring our sense of community." One person was quoted as saying: "Volunteer work has changed my entire outlook on life." Many realize that volunteering can provide a welcome antidote to job stress as well as giving them enormous fulfillment. That's if you know how to get the most from volunteering.

Central Message

Today I want to talk about how you can make your volunteer experience just as enjoyable as possible.

Dialogue Question

Now, I know that some of you are no strangers to volunteer work. Can you tell me what types of volunteer activities you've been doing lately?

(allow audience to describe activities)

Segue & Summary

Each of these is very important. Bill, here, is one of our guides at the Nature Center. Several of you work with Meals on Wheels, and two are Big Brothers. For those of you who may not be involved with a volunteer activity, but who want to get involved, there are a few simple principles that can make your experience more satisfying. Unfortunately, I've had to learn most of them the hard way.

Key Point Pattern

First, think about what you want to do, not what you should do. Before you begin volunteering, ask yourself a question: What interests would I like to pursue that aren't being satisfied through my job or current hobbies? Use the answer as a guide in selecting a volunteer activity.

Personal Anecdote

Once I was asked to join the board of a local charity organization. For years, the whole experience of sitting through board meetings has always been more excruciating for me than the annual visit to my dentist. But against my better judgment, I agreed because it seemed like the right thing to do. Although the organization was doing some wonderful work in this community, my service on the board barely lasted two months. It was simply the wrong thing for me.

Volunteering should give you an opportunity to do something that you want to do. It's a chance to experiment, to broaden your interests and to enhance your repertoire of skills. Whether you succeed or fail, there's not going to be a performance appraisal at the end. The important thing is to learn more about yourself and, perhaps in the process, discover an activity that really excites you.

Dialogue Question

These are only a few of the benefits of volunteering. Would anyone like to talk about some of the benefits that you've received from your volunteer work?

(allow audience to mention benefits)

Segue & Summary

I wish we could talk more on this, but they've only given me a short time to speak today and I don't want to run too long. Some of you mentioned that volunteering enabled you to develop new relationships, to discover a talent you didn't know you had, and to help other people. Now, let's talk about some other ways to make volunteer work satisfying....

Practice Exercise
Develop two open-ended dialogue questions
for the following topics.

1. A new program to encourage telecommuting among employees.

_____

_____

2. A company sponsored wellness program.

_____

_____

3. The benefits of sports for your children.

_____

_____

DIALOGUE QUESTIONS
Develop several dialogue questions for the presentation
which you have been creating.

_____

_____

_____

_____

_____

_____

_____

_____

_____

_____

_____

_____

_____

Questions
& Answers

Another way to encourage audience involvement is through question and answer sessions. These typically occur at the end of a presentation. But if a listener raises a question during the course of your talk, it's best to answer it immediately rather than wait until the conclusion. This not only satisfies your listener, it also increases audience involvement during the body of your talk. Here are several other guidelines to keep in mind for handling Q&A.

1. *Plan ahead.* Some speakers dread a Q&A session because they are fearful of not being able to answer the questions. One way to avoid this problem is to try to figure out in advance which questions the audience is likely to ask, and then you prepare effective responses. Suppose you are talking to a group of employees about the company's plan to change its health benefits program. Given the concern that most people have regarding adequate health insurance coverage for themselves and their families, you could probably anticipate questions such as the following: "Will I be able to continue using my current doctors?" "What about pre-existing conditions, will they be covered under the new plan?" "Will the coverage be just as complete as our current benefits package?" "Are there any additional deductible items or other new costs?" These are the types of issues that listeners are likely to raise in a Q&A session, so you should come prepared to deal with them.

2. *Listen to the question carefully.* Sometimes a speaker will think he knows exactly what a listener is asking and before they finish their question, begin answering it. Interrupting a questioner is discourteous. In addition, the speaker may misinterpret the listener's question and provide a totally inappropriate answer. But even if the speaker has interpreted the question correctly, by answering too quickly he may give a poor response, which might have been

improved if he had given himself a little more time by listening to the entire question.

3. ***Rephrase or repeat the question.*** Another method of buying more time to develop a response is to rephrase the listener's question. In this way, you can give yourself an extra few seconds to think about your answer. During this short time, your brain can process the information more effectively and come up with a more meaningful response. By rephrasing or repeating the question, you also assure the listener that you accurately understand it.

This is especially important for an international audience of listeners who do not have a perfect command of the English language. Make sure you get clarification from the person asking the question because the translation from his native language to English may not be exact; and when you repeat the question back to him, he may realize that he must ask it differently.

The process of repeating or rephrasing a question might go this way. Suppose you are answering a question about the new health benefits package, you might say: "If I understand your question correctly, you want to know if our new health plan will provide any dental coverage for such things as your childrens' braces." Another advantage of repeating a question aloud is that you ensure that everyone else in the audience has heard it. Quite often people in the front of the room, for example, will not be able to hear a question that comes from the back. There is nothing more frustrating than listening to a speaker's response without knowing the question he is trying to answer.

4. ***Learn to handle negative questions.*** A major fear for any speaker, especially if you are talking on a subject considered controversial, is that someone will ask you a "loaded" question. How should you deal with it? If you are prepared for the questions, it will not take you by surprise. But it may not be possible to anticipate everything. By quickly rephrasing a question, however,

you can often neutralize it. This does not mean changing its meaning, which should always be avoided because the audience will
easily see through it and lose confidence in you.

It does mean phrasing the question in a manner that is better suited
to your message. Suppose someone stands up during the Q&A
session following your presentation on the new health care plan
and says: "Companies are always chipping away at our hard-won
benefits, and this sounds like just another example of trying to
take advantage of the employees. Do you want to comment on
that?"

Well of course you don't. But the questioner has probably said
what is on the minds of many other people in the audience. So
you cannot afford to sidestep the question without losing credibility. Suppose you rephrase the question this way: "I think you're
asking whether the new program represents a reduction in our
current benefits." Without changing the meaning of the question,
you have now removed loaded words such as "chip away at our
hard-won benefits" and "take advantage of employees." Although
the question is still a thorny one, it is now far less emotional —
and more neutral — so you can handle it with less difficulty.

5. *Speak to the entire audience.* When you answer a question, do
   not look only at the person who asked it. By addressing the answer to as many people as possible, you keep them in the loop.
   This should not be accomplished, however, by making your answers unnecessarily lengthy. A long-winded response only bores
   your audience, and by the time you finish it, they may have completely forgotten the question. Keep your answers short and to-
   the-point and aimed at everyone.

Another advantage of addressing your answer to the whole audience is that it may effectively shut down a hostile questioner. Suppose you remain riveted on the questioner from the beginning
until the end of your response. Once you finish, if you are still

looking at the questioner, you have given him an opening to ask another hostile question. By looking at a different part of the audience as you complete your answer, you have now given someone else the signal to ask a question. This enables you to exert much greater control over the Q&A session.

6. *At the end of a response, tie it back to one of your major points.* Q&A sessions are not only designed to give your audience an opportunity to gather more information, they should also offer you a chance to reiterate your main ideas, especially your central message. This provides greater focus to the Q&A section of a presentation by enabling you to tie together the entire talk around your key themes. For example, if your central message about the new health benefits package is that it represents an improvement in care for most employees, you should try to reemphasize this point at the end of each of your responses.

Q&A sessions, like dialogue questions, are successful approaches for keeping your audience involved in a presentation. Both of them require careful preparation as well as the ability to think quickly on your feet. Remember, one of the primary goals of any talk is holding the attention of your listeners. For no matter how powerful your ideas may be, they will not have much impact if your audience is not listening to them.

Q&A PREPARATION

Develop several questions that listeners might ask in a Q&A session for the presentation that you have been preparing. Then write your responses to them.

Question

_____

_____

_____

_____

Response

_____

_____

_____

_____

_____

Question

_____

_____

_____

_____

_____

Response

_____

_____

_____

_____

_____

Question

_____

_____

_____

_____

_____

Response

_____

_____

_____

_____

_____

HANDLING THE MEDIA

The prospect of being interviewed by a television reporter is often enough to send cold chills up the spine of even the most intrepid corporate manager. The experience need not bring on an anxiety attack, as long as you just remember that many of the principles that govern Q&A sessions or dialogue questions can also be applied to appearances in front of the media.

Before the interview, you should always try to anticipate the questions you're likely to be asked and set aside some time to prepare adequate responses. Many interviewers begin by asking for background information, then they proceed to some general issues, and finally to the most controversial questions. If the topic is a new factory your company is planning to build, a reporter might start by asking you to explain why the decision was made to construct the facility on this particular site; then, what products the plant will be manufacturing; and finally, several difficult questions about the possibility that your operations will pollute the environment. Of course, some reporters like to ask the toughest questions at the beginning of an interview to throw you off balance, so you should always be ready to deal with the hardest issues first.

By taking a proactive approach to a media interview, you can remain in control of it. Above all, this means recognizing that an interview affords you a unique opportunity to communicate your central message. How? As you respond to each question, tie back your answer to the central message and its meaning for your audience, just as you would in a Q&A session. For example, if you are trying to emphasize that your company's new plant will mean more jobs for the community, keep reiterating this point as you answer each question that the interviewer asks, even the ones about pollution. This will enable you to keep the upper hand.

Audiences are most impressed with logical arguments supported by concrete information. Tell an anecdote or cite an example as you make each point, and do not forget to include some statistics. Reporters love them! If that new factory will generate 2000 additional jobs, say so. Most interviewers are looking for brief sound bites, so make your answers short and meaty and try to avoid long explanations.

One of the cardinal rules of any interview is this: Always be truthful in your answers. Reporters are usually smart, outgoing people who want you to give them a good, honest interview. If you realize during the course of an interview that you have misstated something, go back and correct it. This adds to your credibility in front of the camera. A low-key performance also enhances your credibility. People who are trying to promote their positions too strongly can easily alienate their audiences.

On the day of the interview, a good rule of thumb is to dress conservatively. Any flashy clothes or jewelry will only distract the attention of the audience from what you are saying. A white blouse or shirt usually shines under the hot television lights; blue, on the other hand, is much softer and cooler on camera. Makeup can also improve your appearance on television. A makeup artist can apply a light oil-based powder that will smooth out your skin tone and hide perspiration. Unfortunately, this has an uncomfortable way of appearing just as you are trying to answer a tough question, which may create doubt in the minds of your audience about the veracity of your responses.

Shortly before the interview begins, a microphone will probably be clipped to your jacket or blouse. As you talk and gesture with your hands, avoid hitting the microphone or, if you are sitting in a chair, don't drum your fingers repeatedly on the arm. The microphone picks up all of these noises.

From watching interviews on television, you probably know that in some cases both the reporter and the interviewee appear on camera;

while in others, only the interviewee is seen. In either situation, you should look at the interviewer, not directly into the camera. Once a question has been asked, you may need a few extra seconds to think about it before giving your answer. One way to "buy" a little additional time is by bridging. In this technique, you reflect on the nature of the question before answering it. For example, you might say: "That's a tough question, but I'll try to respond to it," or "I often hear that question...." Remember to keep your answers short and simple, avoiding any meaningless jargon that may confuse your audience.

If you choose not to answer a question, don't simply say: "No comment." This can have a negative impact on an audience, or, even worse, sound as if you're trying to hide something from them. If you prefer not to respond to a question, explain your reason: "You're asking me to predict what might happen next month or next year, and we don't have the facts to do that," or "Several options are currently under consideration, and it would be premature for me to make a public statement at this time."

Should the interviewer ask a highly argumentative question, try to rephrase it in a way that sounds more neutral. Then provide a short answer, tie it back to your central message, and refocus the discussion on this aspect of your presentation. Several years ago CBS news anchorman Dan Rather tried to ambush President George Bush in a famous television interview by asking him a series of controversial questions. But Bush kept returning to his central message, and stating it over and over again, outmaneuvering the wily Rather.

A media interview is simply another forum in which to utilize your presentation skills. With adequate preparation and a clear, focused delivery, you can turn the interview into a valuable tool for communicating your ideas to a wide audience.

Conclusion ─────────────

1. One of the best ways to promote audience involvement is to begin a dialogue with your listeners by asking them open-ended questions.

2. Develop several dialogue questions in advance to be used at various points in your presentation.

3. Another way to encourage audience involvement is through question and answer sessions that typically occur at the end of a presentation.

4. Several important guidelines for successful Q&A sessions include: planning ahead to anticipate the questions likely to be asked; listening to each question carefully; repeating the question after it is asked; handling negative questions by rephrasing them; and speaking to the entire audience when you answer a question.

5. Before a media interview, take a proactive approach and try to figure out the questions that the interviewer may ask you.

6. One of the cardinal rules of any media interview is to always be truthful in your answers.

7. Dress conservatively for the interview and look at the interviewer as you answer the questions.

CHAPTER NINE

ENERGY FOR THE
LONG RUN

Highlights

- *Use energy to develop enthusiasm in your listeners*
- *Vocal skills add energy*
- *Body language also enhances a talk*

Once I listened to a talk on genetic engineering, where so much is currently being done to cure illness and prolong life. The speech was delivered by a friend of mine, who was involved in some of the most fascinating aspects of the field. Unfortunately, his speech contained none of this sense of awe and fascination. In fact, it was a little more than a dry recitation of factual material. After the presentation was completed, he came up and asked me whether I had enjoyed it. I told him that the information was very interesting, but he didn't seem to convey much of the excitement he always expressed whenever we talked about his work together.

"Oh, it's the most exciting field in the world," he said. "But you're not suppose to express any of that enthusiasm when you speak to an audience. They'll think you're being too emotional."

How many speakers have you heard lately who were in danger of showing too much emotion when they talked about their subject?

123

Instead, they usually present their material in a flat, dry speaking voice, with a total air of detachment that gives the impression they are almost completely indifferent to the information that is being delivered. Unfortunately, without any expression of strong commitment from the speaker, the audience is usually unable to generate much interest in what's being said. As a result, the presentation does not stand out and is not remembered because it fails to create any enthusiasm among the listeners.

The best way to develop interest and enthusiasm in your listeners is by using **energy**. Energy can be injected into your delivery vocally with volume, pacing and pauses, and visually with gestures, facial expressions and eye contact. These tools, when properly used, help you present your material in a way that enbles your audience to listen to what you have to say.

        VOCAL ENERGY

We've already mentioned the old adage: "It's not just what you say that's important, but also how you say it." Your style of delivery often determines whether an audience will pay attention to your message and recall it long after you have finished your presentation. If you have any doubt, just contrast the speeches of President Jimmy Carter with those of his successor in the White House, Ronald Reagan. Carter spoke in a slow, halting style that was almost guaranteed to put people to sleep. He seemed almost detached from his words, although he probably believed passionately in what he was saying. Reagan, on the other hand, was a magnificent speaker with a confident delivery. He had an affable speaking style that drew an audience to him and kept them talking about his message long after he had finished his speeches.

One way to improve your delivery and develop a rapport with your audience is to hone your vocal skills. From the time you are born, you learn to use vocal and visual energy. As you enter the world, the doctor slaps you on the rear end and you start to cry and gesture. Almost immediately, we realize that vocal and visual energy are extremely effective ways to get other people to pay attention to us.

An essential aspect of vocal energy is changing the volume of your voice to add emphasis to certain words and ideas. This sends a signal that they are important. In a book like this one, emphasis is added by devices such as headings, italics, and boldface. You do not have these tools when you use your voice. But volume takes the place of them. Here is a brief example from a speech on communications. The words that are underlined show where the speaker added emphasis by changing the volume.

PRESENTATION EXCERPT

As businesses strive to improve their operations through reorganziations, layoffs, and quick changes of direction, many employees are quite justifiably feeling <u>anxious</u> and <u>uncertain</u>. In this type of environment, <u>effective communication</u> is especially important. <u>Good</u> managers should be working even more diligently to <u>enhance</u> their skills rather than laying back and waiting for the business environment to change. This means delivering a message that is <u>consistent</u> and expresses a <u>clear vision</u> of what needs to be accomplished.

Your message should be <u>positive</u> and <u>upbeat</u>, without of course, being misleading. If you're consistently negative about the current state of affairs, it can be extremely difficult to keep employees motivated. Getting the message across to employees is done best if it's delivered <u>verbally and face to face</u>. All studies indicate this is the most <u>memorable</u> and <u>credible</u> way of communicating. It can then be supplemented with printed materials which support the basic message...

Talks delivered without any emphasis and change of volume often seem monotonous because everything sounds the same. By raising the volume at certain appropriate points and adding emphasis, you can put more passion in your delivery. Volume comes from your diaphragm, not your vocal chords. If you only use your vocal chords, you will begin to lose your voice which will not help your delivery.

Another aspect of a successful speaking style is authority. If you put authority in your voice, your audience will be more likely to listen. This does not mean that you should talk down to your listeners. It does mean that you should speak with full confidence that what you are saying is important enough for everyone to pay attention. Confidence comes from adequate preparation of a presentation, mastery of your subject matter, and sufficient practice of your delivery before you stand up in front of an audience. (We will talk about rehearsals in the next chapter).

Effective speakers also know how to use pacing to deliver their message. A close acquaintance of ours, a tax lawyer, addresses an audience at such a speed that it's a wonder anyone can follow him. By contrast, some speakers talk so slowly and quietly that the pace of their presentation lulls an audience to sleep. The best approach is a conversational style of speaking with frequent changes of volume as well as the use of pauses to add emphasis.

The pause — that moment of silence — can be just as powerful as any word you speak when drawing your listeners' attention to the fact that you are about to say something which you want them to remember. Here are a few examples.

1. Today, I'd like to discuss one of the most critical elements of successful meetings (pause): a clear, written agenda.
2. What is the purpose of refocusing our company's sales efforts, you ask? (pause) The competition.
3. This decision will enhance our image in the market place (pause) and that can only mean more sales.

4. Among America's finest companies, we find these features (pause) less hierarchical. They allow more accountability, and push down decision making to the lowest possible level.

A pregnant pause signals that something significant is about to be said, something that you want to make sure your listeners hear. Here is a brief excerpt that shows how combining emphasis together with pauses can enhance your delivery.

PRESENTATION EXCERPT

Perhaps the most difficult problem for anyone writing a business communication is this: (pause) <u>where do I begin?</u> Once you figure out what to put first, what comes next, and what to put after that, a major problem in the writing process is solved. When you read a good piece of writing, the order in which the information is presented seems <u>entirely natural</u>, and you know something? (pause) <u>It is.</u> But that's only because the writer spent time figuring out that order <u>before</u> writing. How do you accomplish this task? (pause) Today, I'm going to talk about several things to keep in mind that will make your next project much more successful....

 VISUAL ENERGY

Experts point out that the way we receive information is 7% verbally, 38% vocally, and 55% visually. Visual aids capitalize on this fact by presenting data in the form of graphs, charts and pictures that appeal to our visual receptors. But, as this book pointed out earlier, you are your own best visual aid. When you are speaking to an audience, they are not only listening to your message but also

looking at you. So your body language becomes a powerful method
of communicating with people and giving them visual stimulation.
But how many of us focus on this aspect of our presentations? One
manager said that he spent "much more time on the verbal than the
vocal and visual." Explaining that he sometimes practices a talk in
front of his family before giving it to a group of colleagues, this
same manager admitted "but I haven't really worked on hand gestures and other body language, which is definitely a weakness."

Since most listeners receive the major portion of their information
visually, it is essential to work not just on what you have to say but
how you deliver it. If you depend on words alone, you will often fail
to reach your audience as well as you might. Get your body involved
in what you are saying — it is a sure way to raise the energy level of
your talk.

Body language involves gestures, facial expressions and eye contact. With a shake of the head, for example, you can indicate dis-
agreement. A smile can show warmth and friendliness. With a raised
eyebrow you can express disbelief or disapproval. But the most valuable tools you possess for adding more impact to your presentations
are your hands. It is very difficult to speak in a low, flat monotone if
you are using your hands to describe basic concepts and reinforce
key points. You will find that your hands seem to take control, putting more power into your voice and enhancing your vocal skills.

If you watch people in a one-to-one conversation, they are frequently
quite animated, relying on their hands to express themselves. But
when they get up in front of a group, these same speakers often stand
with hands at their sides or clasped tightly in front of them. Hands
tend to be heat-seeking and once they come together, it is very hard
to pry them apart. As a result, speakers may stand for almost an
entire presentation in the so-called "fig-leaf" position with hands
locked in front of them. They look as if they're trying to address an
audience from inside a telephone booth, which makes it almost impossible for them to put very much animation into their presentations.

Interviews with managers who take the Focus Communications seminars indicate that many of them are afraid of overdoing their gestures when they deliver a speech. They are so fearful of looking like snake oil salesmen or circus barkers, that they prefer to keep their hands frozen in a single position. However, when they watch videotapes of themselves delivering a presentation, they soon realize that their delivery would benefit enormously from a much greater use of body language.

If you are not someone who regularly relies on gestures to pump more energy into a talk, it may feel uncomfortable at first. Indeed, some students even try to plan their gestures in advance so they will remember to use them. Unfortunately, this often looks very artificial when a talk is being delivered. Instead of a gesture being used at the same time a word is spoken so it can reinforce what the speaker is saying, the gesture may come a little early or a little late. It is almost like watching a movie in which the speaker's words are not properly lip-synched with the movements of his mouth. It looks silly.

Instead, the next time you are supposed to deliver a talk, try to imagine that you are involved in a friendly conversation with one other person. Then let the gestures flow naturally as you talk. If you are discussing your entire department, for example, your hands and arms might naturally move apart in an expansive gesture. If you decide to focus on a single process or procedure, you might begin to jab the air with your forefinger. If you talk about sales in three geographical areas, you might gesture with your hand to the left, then straight ahead, and finally to your right. And if you are talking about the need to increase profits, you might raise your hand above your head. Each of these gestures will serve to enhance your vocal energy. Suppose you're emphasizing the need to raise productivity, for example, you can add even more power with an appropriate gesture. Through your body language, you can communicate a stronger commitment to what you're saying, which not only increases your believability with an audience but also their level of interest in your presentation.

Practice Exercise

What type of body language might you use to make each of the following verbal points in a presentation?

1. Every culture change has to begin in one place — the top.

2. This is the wrong approach to building a business.

3. The New England region, the Mid Atlantic and the Southwest have all shown increases in sales.

4. All of us need to work together on this project to make it a success.

5. Manufacturing looks at the marketplace from one point of view, Customer Service from another.

             EYE CONTACT

Whenever you begin a conversation with someone, one of the best ways of making a connection and establishing rapport is through eye contact. By looking directly into the eyes of the other person, you indicate your interest in that individual and your desire to really communicate. By contrast, if someone is looking away while he talks, you may begin to think that he has no interest in you, or even worse, that he is trying to hide something.

It is the same way when you speak to an audience. If you are constantly looking down at the floor or reading your notes, it indicates a lack of interest in your listeners. By contrast, continual eye contact serves as an extremely valuable visual skill that will help you to telegraph your willingness to engage the listeners in meaningful dialogue. What is the most effective method of maintaining eye contact? Some speakers use a technique called scanning. Their eyes move continually from one person to another as they talk. This approach has serious problems. While the speaker appears to be looking at the audience, his eyes never stay on one listener long enough to really establish a connection with that person. Scanning for a long period of time can also become very tiring for the speaker's eyes.

The most effective way to make eye contact is to select one listener and look only at that individual while you communicate an idea. Once the idea is complete, go on to another person and repeat the process. This approach enables you to be more personal in your delivery, as if you are speaking one-on-one. It also improves your ability to concentrate on what you are saying. You can use this approach with small meetings or large audiences. Suppose a group of people are seated around a conference table listening to your presentation. You might begin by addressing your comments to one listener on the left side, complete a thought, move to another person, then switch to someone on the right. This is usually more effective than bouncing back and forth from one person on the left to one on the right, etc. It is also far less tiring for you.

Visual and vocal skills are an essential part of the speaker's tool kit that enable you to inject more energy into the verbal dimensions of your presentation. Another way of looking at visual and vocal skills is to say that they provide the style which makes the substance so much more meaningful to your audience. As a result, they are crucial to your success.

SPEAKER SURVEY

Evaluate your visual and vocal skills by
answering the following questions about the way
you deliver a presentation.

1. Do you vary the volume in your delivery to add emphasis
   to words and phrases?
   ___often   ___sometimes   ___seldom   ___never

2. Do you use pauses to direct the listeners' attention to an
   important point?
   ___often   ___sometimes   ___seldom   ___never

3. Do you stand with hands at your sides or clasped in front
   of you while you speak?
   ___often   ___sometimes   ___seldom   ___never

4. Do you reinforce your words with appropriate gestures?
   ___often   ___sometimes   ___seldom   ___never

5. Do you use facial expressions to reinforce a point?
   ___often   ___sometimes   ___seldom   ___never

6. Do you look down at the floor or read your notes while
   delivering a presentation?
   ___often   ___sometimes   ___seldom   ___never

7. Do you establish eye contact by looking at one person,
   finishing a thought, and moving on to the next person?
   ___often   ___sometimes   ___seldom   ___never

8. Do you communicate ideas with sincerity, enthusiasm and
   commitment?
   ___often   ___sometimes   ___seldom   ___never

Conclusion ———————————————

1. The best way to develop interest and enthusiasm in your listeners is by using energy.

2. Energy can be injected into your delivery vocally with volume, pacing and pauses.

3. An essential aspect of vocal energy is changing the volume of your voice to add emphasis to certain words.

4. Effective speakers also know how to use pauses to draw the audience's attention to important information.

5. Body language—gestures, facial expressions, and eye contact—is another way to add energy to your presentation.

6. The most successful way to make eye contact is to select one listener and look only at him while you communicate an idea, then go on to another person and repeat the process.

CHAPTER TEN

PRACTICE PAYS OFF

Highlights

- *A rehearsal enables you to perfect your talk*
- *Make sure your central message is clear*
- *Practice your visual and vocal skills*

Whenever we talk to managers who regularly attend presentations, we frequently hear comments like these:

"The visual aids were hard to understand—at least, I couldn't read them from where I was sitting."

"The speaker never seemed to get around to his main point even though he talked for a long time."

"The joke she told in the opening fell flat. Nobody in the audience even laughed at it."

"The speaker never looked at the audience. He was always looking over our heads."

"The talk seemed disorganized. Maybe she should have taken more time to prepare."

For many of us, time often seems to be the most precious commodity we possess. With repeated downsizings, many employees today find themselves doing jobs that used to occupy two or more people in the past. As a result, if you are intending to give a presentation, you may feel fortunate to simply make your deadline. Meanwhile, you have little or no time left over to review your central message and your visual aids, or conduct a dry run to iron out any of the kinks in your delivery. Nevertheless, this extra bit of time can often spell the difference between a good presentation and a mediocre one.

Actors rehearse before they are ready to stage a play in front of an audience, and a great orchestra puts in hours of practice before the day of their performance. Reviews and rehearsals give you a chance to perfect your verbal, visual and vocal skills. This chapter provides a series of checklists and other information that will enable you to evaluate your next presentation before you deliver it so you can avoid some of the most common mistakes that speakers commit.

     ## WHAT IS YOUR ATTITUDE?

The way you approach a presentation says a great deal about how successful it is likely to be. If you look on the talk you are currently preparing as an onerous burden, it will probably color all the work you are doing on it, including the way it is going to sound to your listeners.

On the other hand, if you see it as a unique opportunity to provide the audience with some valuable information, stimulate their thinking, or persuade them of your point of view, you are far more likely to develop a talk that will have great appeal for your listeners, a talk that they will not soon forget. Evaluate the way you have been approaching your current presentation, by answering the following questions:

My Approach to the Presentation

1. Have I been approaching this talk as a burden or an opportunity?
   Burden_____ Opportunity_____
   What else could I do to make the process more enjoyable

   _____

2. Have I been developing a presentation that will appeal to my audience and retain their interest?
   Yes_____ No_____
   What more could I do to make it more memorable?

   _____

   _____

3. Am I going to use the same old style of presenting (keeping my hands locked at my sides, using a pile of overheads, etc.) or am I planning something better?
   Same style_____ Something better_____
   If so, what?_____

 ## WHAT IS YOUR MESSAGE?

The linchpin of every successful presentation is a clear, powerful central message. This should not be confused with your topic. The central message is what you plan to say about the topic. It is a concise statement — only a sentence or two — which is delivered near the beginning of a presentation and repeated periodically throughout, to remind the audience of why you are speaking to them. Each central message should also have meaning or relevance to your listeners, or they will not pay attention to it. Conducting a listener analysis before you give a presentation will enable you to gauge the attitudes of your audience toward the central message and their degree of interest in it, and this way you can make your talk as meaningful as possible. This analysis will also help you determine their level of knowledge about the information you are presenting so you don't speak down to your listeners or over their heads. Review the central message, the meaning of the message, and the rest of the ideas in your presentation to make sure you have incorporated the data gathered from your listener analysis.

My Central Message & Listener Analysis

1. Is the central message a short statement which is easy for my listeners to understand?
   Yes_____ No_____ How can I improve the central message?

   _____

2. How often am I planning to state the central message?
   Only at the outset of my talk_____
   Several times throughout the presentation_____
   Where else could I state it?

   _____

3. Does the central message have meaning for my listeners?
   Yes_____ No_____
   How can I make it more meaningful?

   _____

4. Have I incorporated the data from my listener analysis into the presentation?
   Yes_____ No_____
   What more do I need to do?

   _____

THE STEAK & THE SIZZLE

The strength of your presentation will depend heavily on the information you present and how well it is packaged. Brainstorming for ideas is the first step. Then you must decide which ones directly relate to your central message. Next you need to figure out a way to grab your listeners or they are likely to forget what you have said soon after you leave the podium. Anecdotes, examples and quotations add "sizzle to the steak," making it more satisfying for your audience. A sure-fire way to illustrate a key point is with a good story. By making an abstract idea concrete you ensure that your listeners will hold onto it.

My Sizzle Quotient

1. How many ideas have I put on my Brainstorming Board?
   Few____Some____ Many____
   What other ideas can I add?

   _____

2. Do all of the ideas relate to my central message?
   Yes____ No____
   Which ideas should be eliminated?

   _____

3. Do I have anecdotes, examples, quotes, etc. to illustrate my major points?
   Yes____ No____
   What additional sizzle can I put in my presentation?

   _____

PATTERNS OF SUCCESS

Organizing patterns allow you to arrange information in your presentation so that it flows logically from subject to subject. A familiar pattern also permits your listeners to recognize the connections between your ideas more readily and understand what you are saying more easily. In Chapter Four, we presented several organizing structures: chronological, hierarchical, proposal-benefits, location and key points. Many of them rely on signal words, eg. first, second, next, etc., to alert the audience to the flow of your ideas. When this material is linked tightly to your central message, you have gone a long way to creating a compact and very potent presentation.

My Organizing Pattern

1. What organizing pattern(s) do I use in my presentation?
    _____

2. Does the pattern fit the information which I am presenting?
    Yes_____ No_____
    What other pattern might be more appropriate?
    _____

3. Do I use signal words to indicate this pattern to my listeners?
    Yes_____ No_____
    Which additional signal words should I include and where should
        I put them?
    _____

4. Do I link the organizing structure with my central message?
    Yes_____ No_____
    How could this link be improved?
    _____
    _____

LEAD WITH POWER

Look for the most powerful anecdote, quotation or example that you have collected for your presentation, because this is often the best way to open. If you develop an opening that hooks your audience and relates easily to your central message, you will keep them tuned in to the rest of your speech.

My Opening

1. What type of opening do I have for my presentation?

   _____

2. Is the opening closely tied to my central message?
   Yes___ No___

   How could the opening be more closely related?

   _____

3. Have I kept the opening short and made it punchy?
   Yes___ No___

   How can it be improved?

   _____

4. Have I avoided cliches in my opening?
   Yes___ No___

THE HEART OF THE MATTER

One of the most effective blueprints for presenting an entire talk is the so-called "3Ts". Tell them what you are going to tell them in the opening. Tell them in detail in the body. Briefly tell them what you told them in the conclusion. The body forms the heart of your talk. This is the place to take the organizing structure we discussed earlier and use it to logically present your information. The conclusion should be just as powerful as you can make it, because it is the final word that you are going to leave with your audience. A strong anecdote or quotation works well. But do not forget your central message — it should be restated one last time so no one forgets it.

The Body & Conclusion of My Presentation

1. Do you utilize the 3Ts as a blueprint for presenting your talk? Yes___ No___
   If not, what is your blueprint?

   _____

2. Does the body of your presentation carry out your organizing structure? Yes___ No___
   How could the body be improved?

   _____

3. Do you include all your best anecdotes, examples, quotes, etc? Yes___ No___
   What additional ones might be introduced?

   _____

4. Does the conclusion pack power? Yes____ No___
   How could you improve it?

   _____

A PICTURE IS WORTH
A THOUSAND WORDS

Visual aids bring concepts to life. They show rather than just tell, and a few pictures often carry far more impact than many thousands of words. But only if you know how to use them properly. Too many visuals can overwhelm an audience. Visuals that are too busy can be impossible to read. Garish colors and designs can undercut your central message. Whether you use graphs, charts, word slides or pictures, make sure they are working for, and not against you as you are making a presentation.

My Visual Aids

1. Do I use a minimum of visual aids? Yes___ No___
   Can any of the visuals be eliminated?

   _____

2. Are all the visuals readable? Yes___ No___
   How can they be improved?

   _____

3. Does every visual aid convey only one central idea?
   Yes___ No___
   How can they be simplified?

   _____

4. Do any visual aids contain mistakes in data, spelling, etc?
   Yes___ No___

5. Have I kept the design simple and presented only the necessary information?
   Yes___ No___
   How can the design be modified? _____

AUDIENCE PARTICIPATION

If you want to keep your audience awake, then keep them involved
with open-ended dialogue questions and lively question-and-answer
sessions. Dialogue questions require careful preparation to ensure
that they elicit a response from your listeners. You must also try to
anticipate what questions are likely to arise in a Q&A session so
you can develop convincing answers. It is especially important to
be prepared for any negative questions and to know how to rephrase
and neutralize them. Audience participation is one of the most over-
looked elements of a presentation, and yet one of the most critical to
its success.

My Questions and Answers

1. Are my dialogue questions open-ended and likely to encourage
   audience participation? Yes___ No___
   How could the questions be improved?

   _____

2. Have I developed dialogue questions at various stages throughout the presentation? Yes___ No___
   What additional questions might I include?

   _____

3. Have I thought of the questions that are likely to be asked in a
   Q&A session?
   Yes___ No___
   What other questions might be asked?

   _____

4. Have I developed effective answers for these questions, especially
   negative ones? Yes___ No___
   What improvements could I make to my answers?

   _____

   _____

"Practice is the best of all instructors."
—*Publius Syrus, Ancient Roman Author*

REHEARSAL

Once you finish reviewing various aspects of your presentation, it is time to conduct a rehearsal. This gives you a chance to put everything together and practice your visual and vocal skills. It is a good idea to practice in front of a mirror or to videotape yourself, so you can see how much energy you are putting into the presentation. An even better approach is to conduct a dry run in front of an audience such as your family or a small group of your peers and solicit their feedback. Have them critique the logic and flow of your talk and the clarity of your central message. Ask them to pay particular attention to your visual and vocal skills so they can evaluate your use of gestures and eye contact, emphasis, pacing and pauses. Finally, they should asses your ability to work with visual aids, such as overheads and slides. A rehearsal with feedback will enable you to determine your strengths and weaknesses and to make improvements before you actually step onstage and deliver your presentation.

My Rehearsal

1. What is my energy level? High____ Medium____ Low____
   How can I increase it?

   _____

   _____

2. Do I speak clearly so that all my words are easy to understand?
   Yes____ No____
   What can I do to improve?

   _____

3. Do I establish eye contact with as many listeners as possible?
   Yes____ No____
   How should I change my approach?

   _____

4. How do my gestures appear on the following scale?
   Smooth & Natural   Forced & Inappropriate
      |_____|

5. How does my use of emphasis and pauses rate on the following
   scale?
   Powerful   Ineffective
      |_____|

6. Do I introduce each visual aid by giving an overview and then
   explaining all the details? Yes___ No___
   Where should I make improvements?
   _____

7. Are all the visuals informative and easy to read? Yes___ No___
   Where do I need to make modifications?
   _____

8. Does the presentation carry out the objectives stated in my central message? Yes___ No___
   What changes are necessary?
   _____
   _____

9. Do the ideas in my presentation flow logically? Yes___ No___
   What modifications are needed?
   _____

10. What is the greatest strength of my presentation?
   _____

   What is the biggest weakness?
   _____

11. What is the overall evaluation of my presentation?
    Excellent___   Good___   Fair___   Poor___

Conclusion

1. Reviews and rehearsals give you a chance to perfect your verbal, vocal and visual skills before you deliver your presentation.

2. Evaluate the way you are approaching your current presentation.

3. Define your central message and the meaning of your message and repeat them periodically throughout your talk.

4. Make sure you grab the attention of your listeners with anecdotes, examples and quotations which add "sizzle" to your presentation.

5. Arrange the material in your talk in a pattern that is familiar to the audience.

6. Begin the talk with a powerful opening and utilize the 3Ts as a way of organizing your material.

7. Use visual aids to show rather than tell, but remember that too many visuals will overwhelm your audience.

8. Involve listeners in your presentation with dialogue questions and lively Q&A sessions.

CHAPTER ELEVEN

A WINNING PRESENTATION

Highlights

- *Make sure your talk fits the alloted time*
- *Channel your stage fright into energy for your talk*
- *Check the equipment in advance*

Larry had been invited to be the after-dinner speaker at a management conference for a Fortune 500 company. The vice president for Human Resources had asked him to prepare a thirty minute talk on team-building. But the conference ran much longer than expected, and by the time the participants sat down for dinner, most of them were visibly exhausted. Sizing up the situation from his position at the head table, the vice president leaned over to Larry and asked him to shorten his talk to twenty minutes. Larry smiled and nodded his head. By the time dinner had ended, however, even a twenty-minute talk seemed too long. So the vice president asked Larry to reduce it further. "I think 15 minutes ought to be enough," he whispered.

Finally, Larry was introduced and began his presentation. Fifteen minutes passed, the audience had begun shifting uneasily in their seats, but Larry showed no signs of slowing down. At the 20-minute mark, Larry still had not let up...25 minutes...28 minutes. Apparently, Larry could not, or would not shorten his talk. By the time he finally concluded, at a full 30 minutes, everyone in the audience had mentally checked out long ago. There was not even a ripple of applause as he left the podium — only a collective sigh of relief. The presentation had been a disaster for everyone, including Larry, who was never asked to speak to the group again.

No matter how much time you have spent executing all the steps described in this book, the success or failure of your presentation will often be determined on the actual day you deliver it. An unexpected change in the schedule, an overpowering case of stage fright, an annoying equipment breakdown can undermine hours and hours of work unless you know how to deal with these things effectively. You do not want to stumble as you are approaching the finish line. You want your presentation to be a winner. But this often requires advanced planning as well as some quick, spur-of-the-moment decision-making to ensure that your presentation achieves all of its goals.

Satisfy the customer's expectations.

If you are asked to speak for a specific time period at a conference, always prepare a presentation that fills the bill. A talk that runs too short, may leave the program with an embarrassing hole that is impossible to fill for the conference organizers. But a speech that runs too long may throw the entire program completely off schedule, wreaking havoc for all the presentations and other events that follow you. As a result, your talk may long be remembered not because of the impact of your information or the strength of your delivery, but rather because it created an annoying problem for the individual running the conference.

Sometimes you may find yourself in Larry's situation, asked to cut the length of your presentation significantly because the schedule has changed. How can you do it? First, concentrate on delivering your central message and making it relevant to your listeners. This is the key aspect of your presentation, and one that should be repeated and restated as you talk. Next, pick out two or three principle ideas that support your central message and make sure they are included in your presentation. Then, pare away almost everything else, except a few of the most powerful anecdotes, examples, etc. that will hold your listeners' attention. This type of last minute adjustment may also require you to re-order any visual aids that you were planning to present, discarding those that no longer fit your material. While you may not be entirely thrilled at the prospect of making any of these changes, each of them is usually possible while you still achieve your most important goal: presenting the essence of your talk and giving it as much impact as possible for your listeners.

When in Rome, dress like the Romans.

A business presentation generally requires formal attire, i.e. a suit or dress. But there are exceptions and it is best to find out in advance what is expected of you. One speaker arrived at a conference, dressed in a blue, pin-striped suit, only to discover that everyone in the audience was wearing slacks and a polo shirt. Afraid that the difference in dress might create a barrier between him and his audience, the speaker immediately took off his jacket and removed his tie. Then he began: "Well, now I feel much better...." Everyone immediately felt more relaxed.

Put those butterflies away.

Anxiety is a natural companion for most people who are about to stand up and address an audience. Indeed, a little anxiety can act as a powerful motivator that spurs you on to deliver a powerful performance. But too much of it can leave you weak in the knees and dry in the throat, not exactly the most valuable assets for any speaker who wants to impress a group of colleagues. How do you overcome stage fright? Adequate preparation for a talk helps, but often this is not enough to banish the biggest butterflies. Another approach is to channel your anxiety into the visual and vocal energy that you need to make a successful delivery. Establishing eye contact with one person in the audience as you begin to speak, for example, makes the prospect of talking to an entire group seem less daunting. Redirecting some of your stage jitters

into energy for your gestures enables you to underscore your main
ideas as your anxiety dissipates. Finally, adding volume to your voice
not only allows you to put more emphasis on key words and phrases,
it also scares away some of those inner fears that you may be experiencing. By acting confident, you can usually convince an audience, and, even more importantly, convince yourself that you are a
confident speaker. Once your talk is underway, those initial jitters
will generally disappear and your talk will flow smoothly.

If you leave something out.

Once I spoke in front of a large group about the elements
of effective presentations. After finishing the talk, I suddenly realized that I had completely forgotten to mention
visual aids. But the audience did not seem to know the difference.
Indeed, they gave me a lengthy ovation as I left the podium.

Since the audience generally does not have any advance knowledge
of exactly what you are planning to say, they probably will not realize if you have left something out of your presentation. If your central message, main ideas, and supporting examples are strong enough,
the omission will not seem obvious to them — only to you. Therefore, there is usually nothing to be gained by admitting your over-
sight to the audience and then proceeding to make amends, especially if it means presenting material out of sequence. This will not
only confuse your listeners, it will also undermine your credibility
as a speaker. What's more, the information you omitted is usually
not important enough to affect the overall impact of your talk.

Check your equipment.

When it comes to the equipment necessary for making a
presentation, Murphy's Law always applies. As a result,
you should check out the audio-visual equipment (slide
projectors, overhead projectors, etc.) in advance to make sure it is
working properly. Check that all necessary extension cords are on
hand, that remote control devices are operating correctly, and that
lenses are not scratched or covered with dust. But even these pre-
cautions may not be enough. Bulbs often have a way of blowing out

as you turn on the overhead or slide projector to present your first transparency. It is a good idea to have an extra bulb available when you need it. If you are planning to use video, and you feel the least bit uncomfortable about running the projection system yourself, hire a professional to operate it. Then run the videotape in advance to assure yourself that there are no problems.

You should also test the microphone ahead of time, assuming you are intending to use one. Tap it gently and speak in a normal voice. Some speakers seem to think that they need to talk more loudly into a microphone, but this raises the volume of their voice too high and often distorts it. If a microphone begins to produce feedback while you are speaking, wait for the feedback to disappear before continuing. If it persists, turn off the microphone and rely on the strength of your voice to complete the presentation. Although you may need to speak louder, it is far preferable to trying to compete with the noise coming from a faulty sound system.

What if the audience is not paying attention?

A nightmare for any speaker is to see the audience slip away from your grasp. They start looking at their laps, closing their eyes, or even worse, whispering to each other. How can you deal with this situation? Raise the energy level of your presentation by using your vocal and visual skills. As soon as possible, ask one of your dialogue questions to involve your audience and elicit a response from them. Introduce a compelling example or anecdote as quickly as you can to rekindle their interest in what you are saying. Any or all of these approaches can help to pull your presentation out of the doldrums and re-establish your listeners' interest.

Watch your posture at the podium.

As they address an audience, some speakers stand hunched over the microphone and seem to hide behind the podium. Others appear to be holding onto the sides of the podium for dear life, apparently hoping it will support them under the stress of delivering a presentation. The podium should not be treated as a

security blanket or used as a barrier to separate you from your listeners. If you are speaking from a lectern, do not forget to utilize
your visual and vocal skills. Make eye contact with people in the
audience so you can develop a rapport with them. Instead of allowing your energy to be siphoned off into the podium as you grip it
with all your strength, loosen your hands and use them to gesture as
you speak. Good speakers stand a little bit to one side of the podium so it does not block them from the audience, they speak directly to their listeners, and infuse a high level of vocal energy into
their entire delivery.

Handle those little interruptions.

While interruptions can be disconcerting for any speaker,
you should not let them throw your presentation off track.

Assess each situation as it arises and deal with it in a way
that is best, both for you and your audience. If someone arrives late,
for example, your first inclination might be to express your annoy-
ance. But this only embarrasses the listener, who might have a per-
fectly valid excuse for his tardiness, such as an unforeseen family
emergency. Instead, acknowledge his presence with a smile and continue with your talk. This prevents the flow of information from
being disrupted and keeps your listeners focused on your presentation.

If you are trying to make an important point while refreshments are
being delivered for an upcoming coffee break, it can easily distract
the audience from your talk. In this case, it might be most effective
to briefly acknowledge the interruption and mention that all of you
will be taking a break in a few minutes. Reassured that they will
shortly have a chance to stretch their legs, your listeners will find it
much easier to concentrate for a little longer on your presentation.
Suppose loud talking or the sound from a video projector begins to
be heard from an adjoining room. Instead of trying to speak over it,
which only strains your voice and undermines the impact of your
presentation, stop your delivery momentarily to wait for the sound
to subside. If it does not, ask someone to go next door and request
that the volume be lowered.

Each of these tips will help you deliver a more effective presentation. Once a talk is complete, critiquing your performance can serve as a highly valuable exercise. Every talk presents you with an opportunity to improve your verbal, visual and vocal skills so you can become a more successful communicator the next time you stand up to speak. Remember, great speakers aren't born — they are made through hard work, attention to details, and lots and lots of practice. As you work toward this goal, you will become a more productive employee and a far better leader in your organization.

PRESENTATION EVALUATION FORM
Rate each aspect of your current presentation
on a scale of 1 to 5 (poor to excellent).

1.	Clarity of the central message	1	2	3	4	5
2.	Meaning of the message to the listeners	1	2	3	4	5
3.	Logical flow of ideas	1	2	3	4	5
4.	Effectiveness of anecdotes, quotes, etc.	1	2	3	4	5
5.	Impact of opening and closing	1	2	3	4	5
6.	Dialogue questions with the audience	1	2	3	4	5
7.	Vocal and visual energy in the delivery	1	2	3	4	5
8.	Eye contact with individual listeners	1	2	3	4	5
9.	Handling unexpected events — interruptions, schedule changes, equipment problems, etc.	1	2	3	4	5
10.	Presenting visual aids	1	2	3	4	5
11.	Conducting Q & A sessions	1	2	3	4	5
12.	Overcoming stage fright	1	2	3	4	5
13.	Making improvements over the last presentation	1	2	3	4	5
14.	Receiving a positive response from the audience	1	2	3	4	5

Conclusion ——————————————

1. Satisfy the customer's expectations by preparing a presentation that fits the specific time period you are asked to fill.

2. Dress in attire that is appropriate for your audience.

3. Overcome your stage fright by channeling your anxiety into the visual and vocal energy you need to make a successful delivery.

4. If you leave something out, the omission will probably not seem obvious to your audience.

5. Be sure to check the audio-visual equipment and loud speaker system before you begin your presentation.

6. If the audience does not seem to be paying attention, raise your vocal and visual energy and introduce a dialogue question or an interesting anecdote as quickly as possible.

7. Do not hide behind the podium, stand a bit to one side and speak directly to your listeners.

8. Learn to handle interruptions with finesse.

CHAPTER TWELVE

VIDEO-CONFERENCING & VOICE MAIL

Highlights

- *The key to successful video-conferencing is preparation*
- *Use all the elements of Value Added Communications® in video-conferencing*
- *Energy makes voice mail messages more effective*

At the request of our clients, we have attended a number of video-conferences lately but in almost every case the result has been disappointing. On the television monitor there was often a static wide angle shot of a group of managers seated at a table. Each time one of the managers spoke, you frequently could not tell who was actually doing the talking since the speaker failed to use any gestures or add any energy to his delivery and usually presented his talk in a dull monotone. Some of the people attending the meeting never said a word, so we wondered what they were doing there; while others seemed very disorganized when it was their turn to speak. At the end of the video-conference, there was often no effort made to summarize the proceedings nor was any action plan discussed by the participants. In some cases, we could not even determine why the meeting had been called or what it was designed to accomplish. As someone put it: "The technology may be very impressive, but the meetings are often a colossal waste of time."

157

Video-conferencing is a sophisticated technology which is designed
to save organizations time and money. Instead of putting managers
on an airplane and flying them to a distant location, usually at considerable expense and many lost hours of productivity, these same
managers can now stay where they are and communicate with each
other via television monitors and telephone lines. Video-conferencing
enables managers at various plants to coordinate company-wide programs; it permits salespeople from far-flung territories to review
quarterly sales figures together and plan campaigns to enter new
markets; and it allows company representatives to sit down with
customers thousands of miles away and develop new products to
satisfy their needs.

While the potential of video-conferencing is enormous, the technology is only as effective as the people who are using it. To be successful, managers must know how to prepare for a video-conference. This requires a basic understanding of the video and sound
equipment. Perhaps even more importantly, they must master the
skills of making powerful presentations, the skills which we have
been discussing throughout this book. Finally, they must also know
how to run a successful meeting, one with carefully defined objectives, clear agendas and concrete action plans.

The key to any successful video-conference is preparation
...preparation...preparation. This begins with a general knowledge
of the equipment you will be using. To lead a video-conference,
you do not have to become a video technician, just understand what
the equipment can and cannot do and how to do it. Some companies
have a dedicated video-conferencing room outfitted with cameras,
microphones and monitors. One camera provides a wide shot of
your group, while other cameras capture close-ups of the individu-
als who are speaking as well as any visual aids. Microphones may
be positioned around the table or in the ceiling to pick up everyone's
voice, and monitors display the picture being beamed out as well as
shots of the people from other locations who are participating in the
video-conference.

Many organizations have simpler, portable video-conferencing systems. These consist of at least one camera on top of a monitor. This camera can capture a wide shot of a group or zoom to a close-up of a person who is speaking; an auxiliary camera may also be available to shoot visual aids. With split-screen capability, the visual aid and the person speaking can be displayed simultaneously so the audience can see both of them. Who determines what type of shot — wide, close-up, split-screen — is beamed to the participants at other locations? The meeting leader, utilizing a device called a control unit. For example, this enables you to zoom in for a close-up on a speaker in your group. The zoom works best when it occurs as the speaker is beginning his presentation. Knowing when this is going to happen, however, requires preparation — that is, coordination with the other speakers, and perhaps even a brief rehearsal before the video-conference begins.

If a speaker is planning to project visual aids while he is speaking, this information should also be known in advance so each graph or chart can appear as part of a split screen at the appropriate point in the presentation.

One significant aspect of video-conferencing is that the picture quality is usually not quite as good as the image you are used to seeing on your television at home. In addition, there is a brief but noticeable sound delay between the instant someone speaks and when his audience hears his words at other sites. The reason is that sound has to be coded and compressed for digital transmission, then decompressed and decoded at the other end. This means that you must wait a little longer for your listeners to absorb what you are saying. During free-for-all discussions, you must also wait to ensure that someone at another location has finished what he is saying before you begin talking. Otherwise, you will find yourself interrupting him.

Video-conferencing, like other types of presentations, requires that you use all the skills of Value Added Communications®, such as:

VIDEO-CONFERENCING

Present a clear central message. This is especially critical when you are speaking to colleagues at long distance
and cannot clarify your message as easily as you might
be able to do in a face-to-face meeting.

Make the message meaningful. In a video-conference, the audience is hundreds or even thousands of miles away, far removed from
your presence and with only a video monitor to watch. Everyone
recognizes how readily a television can lull you into a state of pas-
sivity. So it is doubly important that you make your message
relevant to the audience, or you risk losing them very quickly.

Organize your presentation carefully. Select a simple organizational pattern — chronology, key points, etc. — if you are making a
presentation. It also helps if you briefly tell your audience what
information you are planning to cover at the beginning of your talk,
then summarize it again at the conclusion.

Use visual aids. Most of us are accustomed to watching television
programs where the images change rapidly, so anything you can do
to vary the image on the monitor during a video-conference will
provide additional visual stimulation that can hold the attention of
your audience. Video monitors have a 4:3 aspect ratio —horizontal
to vertical — and every visual aid should conform to these guidelines. Designers also advise that you plan each visual aid with at
least a 10% safe area around the margins, or the data will run off the
television screen.

Dress appropriately. Earlier in the book, we presented some guidelines for dressing if you appear on the media. These also apply for
video-conferencing. The most important rule is to dress conservatively, with no flashy clothes or jewelry. Avoid a white blouse or
shirt which will only shine on a television monitor, and select softer
colors such as blue.

Do not forget to use energy. In a cool, passive medium such as television, vocal and visual energy play a critical role in keeping your audience involved in a presentation and preventing the onset of *listener's lethargy.* Gestures, facial expressions, volume and pacing are essential tools that enable you to add impact as you try to communicate with your colleagues thousands of miles away. Energy is especially important when you are speaking as a voice-over for a visual aid. Sometimes this happens when a chart or graph does not appear as part of a split screen but fills the full screen, and you are not seen simultaneously on the monitor. In this situation, a dry monotone can easily cause an audience to lose interest in the visual aid long before you have finished discussing it.

Adjust your speaking style for international audiences. Whenever you speak to people who do not have a perfect command of English, some subtle changes will be necessary in your delivery. You should slow down the rate at which you speak, pronounce your words clearly, and avoid jargon or acronyms which are often confusing. In a recent survey, nearly half of all corporate managers said that people who use business jargon in their presentations are pretentious and unclear. This type of problem is only magnified in video-conferencing where there is a sound delay whenever words are spoken.

In addition, when you speak to international audiences we recommend that you use visual aids that are more pictorial and communicate in a universal language. For example, if you are showing a bar chart that depicts quarterly gasoline sales, you might use little gasoline pumps for each bar instead of simple dark lines. This will ensure that your message is more readily understood by everyone in the audience.

> *"America leads the world not in steel or textiles, but in meetings. The problem is how do you export meetings."*
> *—Robert Half, Corporate Headhunter*

A video-conference is simply a special type of meeting, subject to the same problems that can affect other meetings if they are not run effectively. According to a survey conducted by Focus Communications International, corporate executives often find themselves drowning in a vast sea of meetings, which are often so long and so poorly focused that they cannot accomplish anything worthwhile. Many people who responded to our survey also reported that there is too much superfluous discussion at meetings that is not clearly concentrated on any specific issue. This often leaves participants feeling frustrated, with very little sense of accomplishment. Video-conferences are no exception.

To be successful, a video-conference requires a *clear objective* which must be determined in advance by the conference leader. Otherwise, discussions will meander aimlessly, wasting time and money, with little or no result. Perhaps the objective of the video-conference is simply to share ideas on how to reduce cycle time in the manufacturing process. Or the objective may be to reach a decision on how and when to launch a new product onto the market. In either case, your responsibility as the meeting leader is to make sure that participants at the video-conference stay on track and don't stray from the topic under consideration.

One of the most critical elements of any effective video-conference is a *written agenda*, distributed at least several days in advance by the conference leader. An agenda tells everyone what to expect. It lists the subjects and objectives of the meeting and helps focus the attention of all those attending. The result is that a lot more can usually be accomplished in less time, with fewer digressions and distractions and less wear and tear on everybody involved. Each agenda should be as concise as possible.

As the video-conference leader, it is a good idea to quickly go over the agenda at the start of the meeting. This enables you to summarize the objectives of the conference and preview all the topics that are going to be discussed.

Sometimes last minute events will force you to change your agenda. Be as flexible as possible. Usually if you are well prepared, it is much easier to adjust to any last minute changes. You should announce the change at the outset of the video-conference to help direct everyone's attention to any new development, then proceed with your agenda.

Frequently, topics on an agenda will be discussed by other participants. Another purpose of an agenda is to let them know in advance what will be expected of them. It is very embarrassing for anyone sitting in a video-conference to suddenly be asked to speak on a specific topic and find himself totally unprepared. It is far more useful for each participant to be informed in advance about his role. This role should be just as specific as possible, and each participant in the video-conference should be given sufficient time to prepare. If participants are informed of the overall objective of the conference and how their contribution relates to it, then they will be able to participate much more effectively.

Another way to ensure a successful video-conference is to ***include only those people who are absolutely necessary***. Since a video-conference is cheaper than airplane travel, a leader may often pull extra people into the conference without giving them any clear understanding of what they are doing there. This not only wastes their time but may also bog down the conference in needless discussions that digress from the agenda.

In a study conducted by the Wharton Center for Applied Research of over 200 top-level and mid-level managers, many reported that meetings involved too many people — people who did not make any meaningful contributions to the issues under consideration. Had the participants been limited to only those people directly involved with these issues, the discussion would have been far more effective and much shorter. Each person should also know in advance what role he is expected to play in the conference.

A problem that bedevils many video-conferences is that they often seem to continue far too long. This not only costs money, it strains the patience as well as the concentration of the participants. One of your responsibilities as the conference leader is to *keep the discussion within specific time limits*. You can accomplish this task by applying the guidelines we have just discussed: establishing a clear objective, developing an agenda in advance, and limiting the number of participants.

Many video-conferences seem to suffer from a lack of closure. What they need is an *action plan*. In the survey developed by Focus Communications International, more than half the respondents indicated that an action plan is only sometimes, or worse yet, seldom developed from the decisions made at video-conferences or other meetings. Indeed, participants often leave a conference without being certain what decisions were made or how to carry them out. As a result, the video-conference achieves very few concrete results. By contrast, an action plan clearly sets out what everyone is expected to accomplish in order to achieve a set of agreed-upon goals.

Developing an action plan is usually the responsibility of the conference leader. As the leader, you should have a pretty firm idea of why you are holding the video-conference and the goals you hope to reach. During the conference, itself, keep track of the decisions being made that relate to each goal and the actions that will be necessary to carry them out. Near the end of the conference, you should try to summarize what has occurred and ask for feedback from the other participants to ensure that your summary is accurate. Finally, you and the other participants can decide who should be responsible for each action and establish a reasonable time frame in which to execute it.

Once the action plan is set in motion and the video-conference is concluded, your responsibility as the conference leader is still not complete. You need to *follow up* and ensure that all the decisions are being successfully carried out. If any problems arise that threaten to throw off your timetable, you should be aware of them and participate in finding solutions. This is the best way to clearly demonstrate your commitment to the action plan.

A final important step in video-conferencing is to ***evaluate the conference***. After the participants have a little time to reflect upon the experience, ask them to send you their comments, via fax or e-mail. These will enable you to make any necessary changes that might improve the next video-conference. Here is a form that will help you in conducting your next video-conference.

VIDEO-CONFERENCE

OBJECTIVE

_____
_____
_____
_____

AGENDA

_____
_____
_____
_____
_____
_____
_____

PARTICIPANTS

_____
_____
_____
_____

ACTION PLAN

_____
_____
_____
_____

FOLLOW UP

_____
_____
_____
_____
_____
_____

OVERALL CONFERENCE EVALUATION

_____
_____
_____
_____
_____

VOICE MAIL

When a large New York investment firm held a training program for its salespeople, the guest-speaker was a dynamic young woman who manages one of America's premier mutual funds. As part of her presentation, she told of receiving at least one hundred and fifty voice mail messages every day, mostly from salespeople like those in the audience who were telling her about some investment opportunity. The fund manager admitted that she ignored most of these messages, and only a select few warranted her response. Which messages were they? Those that got to the point right away and presented timely, accurate information which she could use immediately.

Today, many telephone calls no longer consist of a conversation between a caller and a receiver in which two people interact with each other. Instead each person may simply leave a message for the other or trade a series of messages back and forth without ever having a real dialogue. In this process of "telephone tag," the caller must respond to an impersonal sounding recorded voice usually followed by a high-pitched beep. Salespeople, like the brokers in our example, know that when they make these calls their messages must vie with scores of similar messages left by their competitors. How, then, do they stand out? How do they distinguish themselves from everyone else?

One way is to use the verbal, vocal and visual skills which we have been discussing in this book and apply them to voice mail. As the mutual fund manager explained, she responds to messages that get to the point quickly and provide her with relevant information. In other words, the central message must be clear and it must be meaningful to the listener. This is essential in voice mail where you may have only a limited amount of time to speak and your listener may receive a large number of similar messages each day.

Developing a clear central message takes a little preparation. It should be succinct, easily stated in a few words, and delivered at the beginning of your voice mail communication. If you meander too long before getting to the point, your listener is likely to push fast forward and go on to the next voice mail message. The voice mail should also have direct meaning or relevance to the listeners. Otherwise, they probably will not respond to it. The meaning of the message should also be stated as soon as possible so that you grab the attention of the listener very early in the voice mail communication.

Here is an example: "I have just received some information on managed health care firm, XYZ, that will make it an excellent investment opportunity for your mutual fund. We expect an annual return of 16%. Please call me as soon as you can to discuss the details."

Vocal and Visual Skills.
What you have to say is a key element of any communication, but, as we have explained throughout this book, the way you deliver it is equally important. We worked with a group of salespeople who spend many hours each day on the telephone. We asked them to record a typical voice mail message, then play it back and listen to it. Most of them said that their voices sounded tired, uncertain, unenthusiastic and bored with the information that they were delivering. Imagine how their listeners must react to hearing these same dull voices over and over again!

Voice mail presents a tremendous challenge for any communicator. You must speak to dead silence and empty space. No matter how enthusiastic you may feel about your message, it is difficult to maintain the same level of enthusiasm when your are receiving no response from anyone at the other end of the telephone line.

Humans are by nature social animals, and when we speak we expect others to listen and react to us. None of this occurs when you deliver a voice mail message. Nevertheless, if you communicate without any energy in your voice, rest assured that most listeners will press that fast forward button and forget about your message.

In Focus Communications training programs, we encourage participants to use a headphone and speaker set when they talk, instead of the typical telephone. This enables them to have both hands free when they speak. By using their hands to gesture, speakers can inject far more energy into a verbal communication. It is almost impossible to speak in a lifeless monotone when your hands are moving. Most people use their hands expressively when they are having a one-to-one conversation with a friend or colleague. By pretending to speak to someone sitting right in front of them, each participant in our program learns to use gestures more effectively in a voice mail communication. Facial expressions are another way to add energy. At first, it may sound somewhat unusual to imagine yourself using a smile or a raised eyebrow as part of your delivery over the telephone. But frequently you do these things anyway even without being aware of them. By making facial expressions a regular part of your delivery, you can give your communication greater impact by adding feeling to your voice.

Vocal skills are important, too. If your voice mail message is not infused with confidence and commitment, you cannot expect anyone else to take it too seriously. How many times do you hear a voice message in which the speaker's voice sounds lifeless and indifferent, as if he is only repeating a prepared script with no real interest in it? By increasing the volume at certain points and putting emphasis on certain words, you can add more energy to your message.

Pacing is also useful. You can slightly increase the tempo of your delivery over some sections of a voice mail communication, then slow down as you reach the most critical information. Listeners notice these changes and pay more attention to your message. Pauses signal the fact that you are about to say something especially significant, something that your listener is sure to find extremely relevant.

Following is an example of a voice mail communication in which the speaker presents the central message and the meaning of the message very succinctly while also adding energy by using pauses, pacing and emphasizing specific words.

PRESENTATION EXCERPT

Hi, Bob, it's Jim Carlton calling. **(slows the pace)**
Have you ever thought that voice mail should have a
greater impact in your business? **(pause)** How? By
teaching your salespeople to use their <u>visual</u>, <u>verbal</u>,
and <u>vocal skills</u> more effectively. Why don't you give
me a call and we'll talk about it.

Practice your voice mail delivery by recording your message to a
listener and evaluating it according to the following check list:

Central Message/Meaning of the Message:
☐ Stated early in the communication
☐ Succinct
☐ Easy to understand
☐ Relevant to the listener

Visual Skills:
☐ Adding energy with gestures
☐ Using facial expressions

Vocal Skills:
☐ Speaking with confidence
☐ Varying the pacing
☐ Changing volume
☐ Using pauses for emphasis

The skills we have been discussing in this book can be used in a
wide variety of situations, such as making presentations to large
groups, one to one disucssions, video-conferencing and voice mail.

By honing your verbal, visual and vocal skills, you can become a better speaker which not only enhances your overall professionalism but also increases the effectiveness of your entire organization.

If you have any questions or need any help with your next presentation, please call us at Focus Communications, International, (203) 966-0282. Good luck and good speaking.

Conclusion

1. Successful video-conferences require an understanding of the video and sound equipment, a mastery of the skills for making powerful presentations, and a knowledge of how to run effective meetings.

2. When speakers appear on camera they must remember to present a succinct, meaningful central message, use visual aids to vary the television images, dress conservatively and use energy in their delivery.

3. Video-conference leaders should also define a clear objective for the meeting, prepare a written agenda in advance, include only those people in the conference who are absolutely necessary, keep the discussion within specified time limits, and present an action plan to be executed after the conference is completed.

4. Today many telephone calls no longer consist of a conversation between a caller and a receiver, but a voice mail message.

5. These messages will have much more impact if speakers use verbal, visual and vocal skills in their communications.

PLANNING EXERCISE

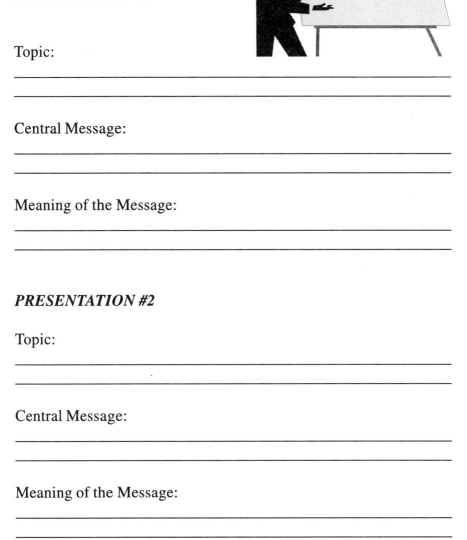

PRESENTATION #1

Topic:

_____

_____

Central Message:

_____

_____

Meaning of the Message:

_____

_____

PRESENTATION #2

Topic:

_____

_____

Central Message:

_____

_____

Meaning of the Message:

_____

_____

PRESENTATION PLANNER

Week #	*Planned*	*Accomplished*
Monday		
Tuesday		
Wednesday		
Thursday		
Friday		
Weekend		

IDEAS AND INFORMATION

IDEA _____

    QUOTE _____

_____

_____

        SOURCE _____

    EXAMPLE _____

_____

_____

_____

        SOURCE _____
    ANECDOTE _____

_____

_____

_____

        SOURCE _____

    STATISTICS _____

_____

_____

_____

        SOURCE _____

    FACTS _____

_____

_____

_____

        SOURCE _____

OUTLINE FOR YOUR PRESENTATION
1. Central Message 2. Meaning of the Message
3. Main Ideas 4. Supporting Information

_____
_____
_____
_____
_____
_____
_____
_____
_____
_____
_____
_____
_____
_____
_____
_____
_____
_____
_____
_____
_____
_____
_____
_____
_____
_____
_____
_____
_____

OPENING FOR YOUR PRESENTATION

Write an opening for the presentation which you
outlined in the previous chapter.

_____

_____

_____

_____

_____

_____

_____

_____

_____

_____

_____

_____

_____

_____

_____

_____

_____

_____

_____

_____

_____

_____

_____

_____

_____

_____

_____

_____

_____

_____

Practice Exercise

Practice organizing the opening and the body of a talk into brief notes with one of the following examples:

1. The advantages of living in your community.
2. How to be an effective volunteer.
3. The process of finding a new job.

Opening

_____

_____

_____

_____

_____

_____

_____

Section I

_____

_____

_____

_____

_____

_____

Section II

_____

_____

_____

_____

_____

_____

CONCLUSION FOR YOUR PRESENTATION

Write the notes for the conclusion to the presentation
which you have been developing.

_____

_____

_____

_____

_____

_____

_____

_____

_____

_____

_____

_____

_____

_____

_____

_____

_____

_____

_____

_____

_____

_____

_____

_____

_____

_____

_____

_____

_____

_____

VISUAL AID PLANNER
Develop the visual aids for the presentation that
you have been creating.

MAIN IDEA	VISUAL
1.	
2.	
3.	

Practice Exercise
Develop two open-ended dialogue questions
for the following topics.

1. A new program to encourage telecommuting among employees.

_____

_____

2. A company sponsored wellness program.

_____

_____

3. The benefits of sports for your children.

_____

_____

DIALOGUE QUESTIONS
Develop several dialogue questions for the presentation
which you have been creating.

_____

_____

_____

_____

_____

_____

_____

_____

_____

_____

_____

_____

_____

_____

_____

_____

_____

_____

_____

_____

_____

_____

_____

_____

_____

_____

_____

_____

_____

_____

Q&A PREPARATION

Develop several questions that listeners might ask in a Q&A session for the presentation that you have been preparing. Then write your responses to them.

Question

_____

_____

_____

Response

_____

_____

_____

Question

_____

_____

_____

Response

_____

_____

_____

Question

_____

_____

_____

Response

_____

_____

_____

GLOSSARY

Brainstorming Board — This is a central location where you can collect all of your ideas for a presentation.

Central Message — This is the theme of a talk, that is, the reason why you are speaking to your audience.

Dialogue Questions — These are open-ended questions inserted at various points in a presentation to promote audience participation.

Listener Analysis — This is an evaluation of the attitudes and knowledge of your audience as well as their positions in the organization.

Listener's Lethargy — This occurs as a listener loses interest in a talk and begins to daydream.

Meaning of the Message — This refers to the relevance or importance of the central message to the audience.

Organizing Patterns — These are common structures for organizing a presentation, such as chronology, location, and key points.

Verbal Skills — The content of your talk: these include defining the central message of your talk, conducting research, developing the main ideas, creating visual aids, and handling question and answer sessions.

Video-conferencing — A sophisticated technology that uses television monitors, satellites, and telephone lines to enable managers to meet without traveling.

Viewgraph — This is another name for an overhead transparency, or foil.

Visual Skills — These refer to the effective use of gestures and facial expressions to reinforce your words.

Vocal Skills — These include pacing, pauses, and changes of tone and volume as you deliver your presentation.

BIBLIOGRAPHY

Axtell, Roger. *Do's and Taboos of Public Speaking.* New York: Wiley, 1992.

Bennis, Warren. *On Becoming a Leader.* Reading, Mass: Addison-Wesley, 1989.

Brown, David. *I Would Rather Be Audited By the IRS Than Give A Speech.* Dubuque: Kendall/Hunt, 1995.

Conger, Jay. *Learning to Lead: The Art of Transforming Managers into Leaders.* San Francisco: Jossey-Bass, 1992.

Cooper, Morton. *Winning with Your Voice.* Hollywood, Florida: Fell, 1990.

Eccles, Robert and Nitin Nohria. *Beyond the Hype: Rediscovering the Essence of Management.* Boston: Harvard Business School Press, 1992.

Hammer, Michael and James Champy. *Reengineering the Corporation.* New York: HarperCollins, 1993.

Hedricks, William, Micki Holliday, Recie Mobley, and Kristy Steinbrecher. *Secrets of Power Presentations.* Franklin Lakes , New Jersey: National Press Publications, 1996.

Hill, Linda. *Becoming a Manager: Mastery of a New Identity.* Boston: Harvard Business School Press, 1992.

Hinkle, Sue. *"Not Just Another Pretty Face: 10 Tips for The Most Effective Use of Type."* Prentations, January, 1995

Hoff, Ron. *I Can See You Naked.* New York: Andrews & McMeel, 1992.

Jeary, Tony. *Inspire Any Audience.* Dallas: Trophy Publishing, 1996.

Kotter, John. *The Leadership Factor.* New York: Free Press, 1988.

185

Leech, Thomas. *How To Prepare, Stage, and Deliver Winning Presentations.* New York: Amacom, 1992.

O'Meara, Frank. *"The Trouble With Transparencies."* Training, May, 1995.

Muuter, Mary. *Guide to Managerial Communications.* Englewood Cliffs: Prentice Hall, 1992.

Pearce, Terry. *Leading Out Loud.* San Francisco: Jossey-Bass, 1995.

Pearson, Latresa. *"Wake Up Your Overheads."* Presentations, March, 1994.

Rabb, Margaret. *The Presentation Design Book.* Chapel Hill: Ventana Press, 1993.

Senge, Peter. *The Fifth Discipline.* New York: Doubleday, 1990.

Walton, David. *Are You Communicating?* New York: McGraw-Hill, 1989.

INDEX

A

Anxiety, 151-152
Appendix, 173-182
Attire, 151, 160
Audience participation, 109-118, 144
  dialogue, 109-112
  dialogue questions, 113
  listener's lethargy, 14, 153, 161
  practice exercise, 113
  presentation excerpt, 110-113
  Q&A sessions, 114-117
  Q&A preparation, 117-118

B

Body language, 128, 130
Body (presentation), 76-87
Brainstorming, 28-30, 139
Brainstorming board, 30, 33

C

Central message (presentation), 14-19,
  137-138, 139
Charts (see visual aids)
"Cs" (seven), 9-10
Conclusion (presentation), 88-89

D

Dialogue questions, 113

E

Equipment, 152-153
Energy
  vocal, 124-127, 161
    presentation excerpt 125, 127
  visual, 127-129, 161
    practice exercise, 130
Eye contact, 130-131

F

Focus Communications International, ix,
  xi, xiii-xiv, 6, 23, 129, 168

G

Graphs (see visual aids)

I

Interruptions, 154

L

Listener analysis, 20-22, 138
Listener's lethargy, 14, 153, 161

M

Meetings, 96-97
Media, 119-121

187

O

Organizing patterns, 42-59
  chronology, 43-47
  combination, 57-58
  hierarchical, 49-51, 81
  key points, 54-57
  location, 47-49
  proposal-benefits, 52-54, 81
Outlines, 58-59

P

Posture, 153
Presentations
  attitude toward, 136-137
  audience attention to, 28, 153
  body of, 76-87
  central message of, 14-19, 137-138, 139
  "Cs" (seven), 9-10
  conclusion of, 88-89
  evaluation form, 155
  excerpts from, 35-39, 82-84
  listener analysis, 20-22, 138
  opening of, 61-72, 141
    anecdotes & examples, 65-66
    central message, 70
    questions, 68-69
    quotations, 67
    statistics, 68
  organizing, 41-58, 140
  outline of, 58-59
  planning of, 23-25
  planner, 25
  purpose of, 3
  rehearsal of, 145-146
  "Ts" (three), 76-77, 90, 142
  time limits of, 150-151
Presentation Evaluation Form, 155

Q

Q&A (presentation evaluation), 11-12

S

Speaker survey, 132

T

"Ts" (three), 76-77, 90, 142
Tables, (see visual aids)

V

Value Added Communications, ix, x, 157, 159
Verbal skills, 4
Viewgraph, 103
Video-conferencing, 157-166
  action plan, 164
  clear objective of, 162
  evaluation of, 165
  follow up, 164
  time limits of, 164
  written agenda of, 162
Visual aids, 92-106, 143
  bar graphs, 98-99
  central idea, 93
  formats, 102-105
  line graphs, 101
  pie charts, 100
  planning, 93
  tables, 97-98
  types of, 94-95
Visual skills, 4, 168-171
Vocal skills, 4, 168-171
Voice mail, 166-171
  presentation excerpt, 170
  vocal and visual skills of, 168-171

AVAILABLE AT YOUR FAVORITE BOOKSTORE!

**The Greatest Salesman
In The World**
Og Mandino

This is the best-selling inspirational and sales book in the world. It contains the Ten Greatest Scrolls For Success.
13,000,000 million copies sold!

ISBN: 0-8119-0067-3 . . .$14.95

**When the Other Guy's
Price Is Lower**
James M. Bleech, Dr. David G. Mutchler

"This book is a winner ... destined to lead the sales profession into the 21st Century! It shows how to outsell the competition — even when the other guy's price is lower."
— Og Mandino

ISBN: 0-8119-0811-9 . . . . . .$14.95

No Bull Selling
*Now You Can Gain the Secrets
of Super Sales Success*
Hank Trisler

"This book has enough down-to-earth information and ammunition to make you as good a professional salesperson as you want to be." **— Og Mandino**
ISBN: 0-8119-0765-1 . . $12.95

**How To Choose A Career Now
That You're All Grown Up**
Anna Mae Walsh Burke, Ph.D., J.D.

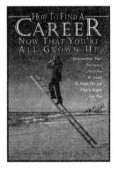

"This step-by-step guide shows how to: explore your life and interests; identify new career goals; get a job after a lifetime of school; save money on counselors, head hunters and resume writers."
—Money Lines Magazine
ISBN: 0-8119-0804-6 . . . . . $14.95

Place Orders: Lifetime Books, Inc.
1-800-771-3355, ext. 14 • Fax: 1-800-931-7411
Credit Card orders accepted
(Visa, MasterCard, Amex)

AVAILABLE AT YOUR FAVORITE BOOKSTORE!

The Psychology of Relationship Selling
Developing Repeat and Referral Business
Orv Owens, Ph.D.

Learn to master the use of psychology to achieve sales success. "Orv Owens offers a winner."

— Og Mandino

ISBN: 0-8119-0832-1 . . .$14.95

Create And Manage Your Own Mutual Funds
Vita Nelson & Donald J. Korn

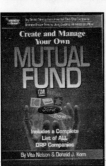

This is for the "little guy" who wants to invest but can't afford to risk his life savings. Contains a listing of all 900 U.S. companies offering DRPs.

ISBN: 0-8119-0773-2 . . $15.95

How To Be The Complete Professional Salesperson
Robert L. Shook

A bestselling author whose 36 previous books total 5 million copies, offers tips, strategies and examples on how to become the best salesperson

ISBN: 0-8119-0792-9 . . . . . .$12.95

How To Get Rich And Stay Rich
Fred J. Young

Over 250,000 copies sold! *"A step-by-step method of acquiring wealth without risks."*

— Naval Association News

ISBN: 0-8119-0491-1 . . . . . $12.95

Place Orders: **Lifetime Books, Inc.**
1-800-771-3355, ext. 14 • Fax: 1-800-931-7411
Credit Card orders accepted
(Visa, MasterCard, Amex)